Military Writers Society of America

Gettysburg Writers' Retreat

May, 2016

Battlefield B&B

Copyright: 2017 Pat McGrathAvery and Joyce Faulkner

All Rights Reserved. No part of this book may be reproduced or transmitted in any form or by any means, electronic or mechanical, including photocopying, recording, or by an information storage and retrieval system (except by a reviewer who may quote brief passages in a review to be printed in a magazine, newspaper or on the Internet) without permission in writing from the publisher.

Library of Congress Control Number: 2017932457

ISBN: 978-1-943267-34-7

Red Engine Press
Pittsburgh, PA

Printed in the United States.

Dedication

While the focus in this book is the Battle of Gettysburg, we dedicate it to all the men and women in our military and to their families. It is a profession that takes a toll from those who take the oath—be they fallen, wounded, or fortunate enough to have moved on in a world that frequently forgets their service. Estimates put the casualties from the Battle of Gettysburg alone at over 50,000 men. These men didn't start the war nor did they create the moral or economic conflict that did. Today, more than 150 years since that horrific battle, our men and women still step forward to serve, and they still make the ultimate sacrifice.

We thank them and wish them peace.

Bob Doerr

Photo by Pat McGrath Avery

Photo by Pat McGrath Avery

Foreword

Gettysburg! I first heard the name of that place during my early school years. I knew there had been a major battle there between the North and the South during the Civil War, and I knew about Lincoln's inspiring Gettysburg address. It took a well-planned writers' retreat sponsored by the Military Writers Society of America (MWSA) for me to sense the pulse of Gettysburg and to enter into the continuous stream of people wanting to have the feeling of being there.

My first impression of this special place came from the rolling fields and high ridges densely populated with more small and large monuments than I had ever seen anywhere else, completely out of place in such a rural setting. Learning of the clashes and military units marked by those monuments was the inhaled essence of history.

I walked through Soldiers National Cemetery, stood where Lincoln gave his address, and then chose a random name from a gravestone as an assignment to learn more about someone who fought there. The results of my study appear elsewhere in this book.

I was the novice history buff, new to Gettysburg but not to history with my New England background. Others in our group had visited Gettysburg many times, learning a bit more on every trip and saturating themselves with the atmosphere as they hiked the route of Pickett's Charge or climbed Little Round Top. Some were established historians while others tasted for the first time the meat of events that predated their grandparents' generation.

The resulting essays of our group await you in this book. Gettysburg: a place, a battle, a turning point in the war that killed and wounded more Americans than any other. It took many decades to heal the physical, mental, and spiritual wounds of that battle and war. Hopefully, Americans will never have to survive three Gettysburgian days again.

Richard Davidson

Photo by Pat McGrath Avery

Table of Contents

Elliott's Map - Joyce Faulkner 1

Thoughts on a Common Soldier - Mindy Phillips Lawrence 17

The Wait - Joe Epley 21

I Will Not Be a Number - Richard Davidson 29

The Sixth Copy - Florence March 39

Living in the Shadow - Florence March 43

Reunion - Carolyn Schriber 49

Understandings - Christopher Avery 63

A Cousin's Promise - Dwight Jon Zimmerman 73

Retreat - Pat McGrath Avery 83

Two Points of View - Bob Doerr 87

The Ghost Stuff - Luke the Detective Dog 97

An Uncivil War - Jack Woodville London 101

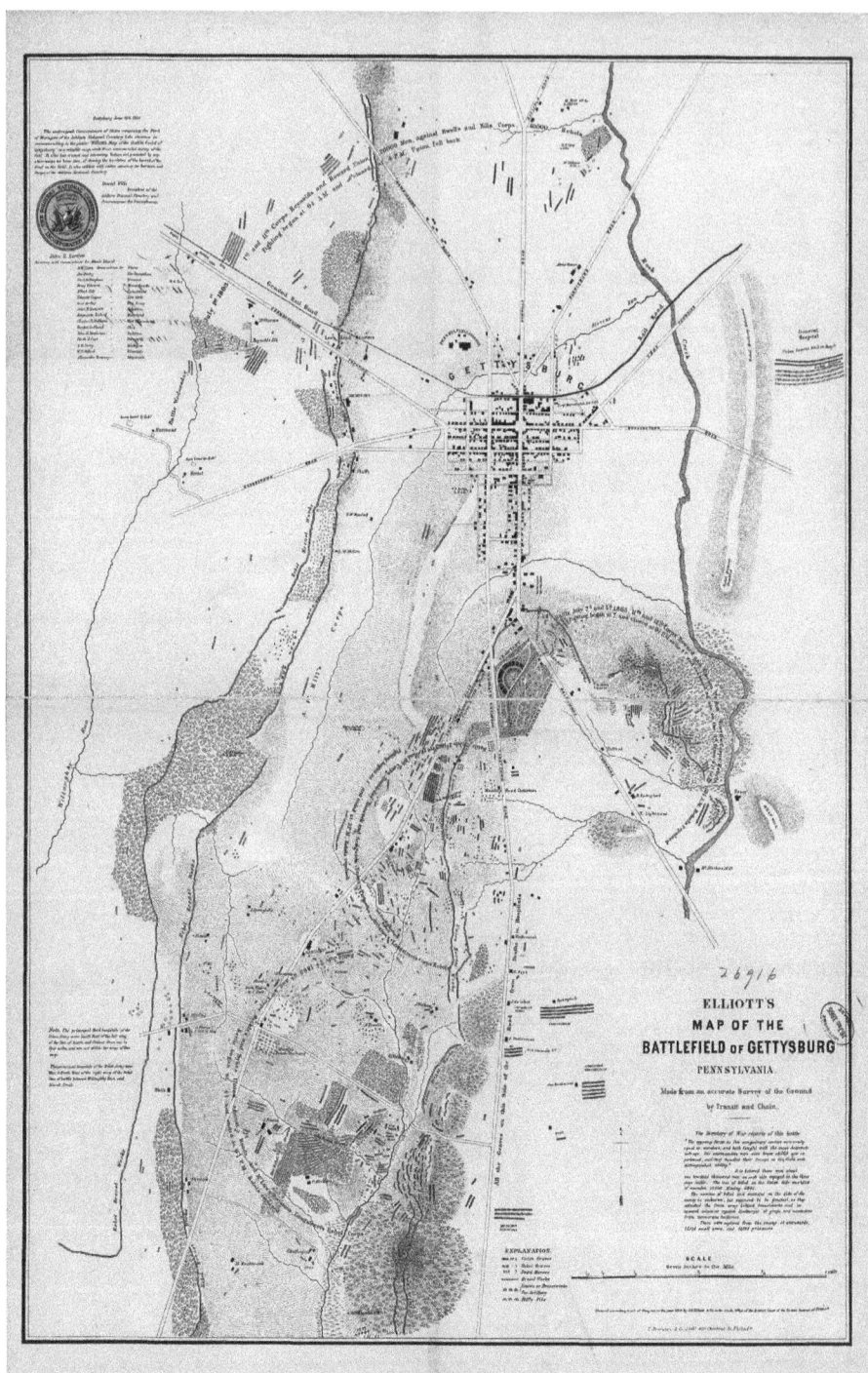

ONE

Elliott's Map

Joyce Faulkner

Whenever I visit Gettysburg, I go to the Angle and ponder. Sitting on a rock with a light breeze in my face, I enjoy the lush Pennsylvania countryside as it slopes across acres of farmland to a line of trees on Seminary Ridge. On a sunny spring afternoon a century and a half after the battle, it's hard to imagine the tragedy that played out on the grassy theater around me—the infamous and unsuccessful assault commonly known as 'Pickett's Charge.' I sniff the air. It smells of desperation and foolhardiness now. Then, that very same scent might have been labeled determination or courage.

I close my eyes and the souls of the soldiers who died here rush through me. It's a moment when time collapses—and past and present merge. I shiver—visualizing the bodies they left behind, scattered across the landscape around me. The history of this place, I realize, is only part of a grand saga that still has the power to move us today.

At the end of the three-day battle on July 3, 1863, Gettysburg and the farms around it were overwhelmed with casualties from both armies. During the fight, the weather had been hot and the stink of death filled the noses of participants and witnesses alike. And then it rained the next day. The exhausted combatants hunkered down in their respective positions until the evening of July 4, when the Confederate Army withdrew.

During the lull before the retreat, soldiers short on food, shoes, weapons, ammunition, and other supplies took what they could from the bodies of their comrades. A friend might retrieve a dead soldier's soggy bible. A brother might snip a lock of hair from his fallen sibling to take home to his soon-to-be-grieving mother. A father might scrawl a name on a piece of paper and pin it to the jacket of a beloved son. Passersby might take that same jacket an hour later, leaving the identifying note to dissolve into the mud. Barefoot boys took wet shoes from those who no longer needed them. Men with worn-out pants stole less worn-out trousers—whether they were blue or gray.

Gettysburg has a high water table which causes basements to flood and fields to become sodden. For the incapacitated, drowning was a possibility

— and infection. As the South retreated, leaving thousands of dead men and horses behind, Northern military doctors and citizens focused on the living first.

On July 5, the summer heat returned. Decay obscured individual identity first, then rank and then even whether the dead, in life, fought for the North or the South. Citizens gagged and threw dirt over corpses to reduce the stench, disease—and the horror of animal predation. Soon battlefield records were the main clues to where almost 8,000 people were buried in the farmland around Gettysburg.

John W. C. O'Neal

During and after the battle, Dr. John W. C. O'Neal, the Adams County Physician, treated wounded soldiers from both sides. As he traveled around the community, he took notes describing the corpses he saw—including names when possible, army units, and specific locations. Several other citizens, most notably Samuel Weaver, a local businessman and photographer, also explored the battlefield and documented the location of graves. Motivated by humanitarian concerns, these men believed that the families of men killed on both sides would need this information to find their loved ones at the end of the war. Their early work continues to support historic inquiries even today.

MWSA Authors

Sketch artist Alfred Waud, photo by Timothy O'Sullivan

In addition to the efforts of Dr. O'Neal and Samuel Weaver, journalists like Mathew Brady and his team recorded the ghastly images. Twenty-three-year-old photographer, Timothy O'Sullivan, spent days shooting pictures of the battlefield. "Confederate dead gathered for burial at the southwestern edge of the Rose woods, July 5, 1863" is one of his most memorable images from the second day of fighting at Gettysburg. Even today, it is possible to identify from O'Sullivan's photographs where certain groups of bodies fell based on their proximity to well-known landmarks like Rose's Woods.

When I first saw O'Sullivan's pictures, I studied the faces of the corpses carefully. My great, great uncle fought with the 8th South Carolina, Kershaw's Brigade, McClaws Division. It was silly really. His unit fought first in the Peach Orchard and then the Wheatfield where he died. What were the chances that his body had been moved to Rose's Woods for burial? And besides, I've never seen a picture of him. Still, what if he was buried near Rose's Woods? Surely it is possible. My anxiety about a man I never heard of until a few years ago—who died long before my grandfather was born—gave me an inkling of the importance of historical documentation.

MWSA Gettysburg Writers' Retreat

Gettysburg, Pa. Confederate dead gathered for burial at the southwestern edge of the Rose woods, July 5, 1863, Photo by Timothy O'Sullivan

The treatment of the Gettysburg dead varied based on their allegiance in life. Federal combatants and local citizens viewed Confederates as traitorous invaders. Union soldiers were patriots and heroic defenders. Bodies wearing gray were buried in mass graves and forgotten. The Union Army and civilians living in the area took more care with those wearing blue.

In October of 1863, Samuel Weaver accepted a contract to dig up Union bodies and move them to the new National Cemetery. He subcontracted the work to freeman Basil Biggs and his crew of black laborers. Together, they explored known sites and opened all the graves they found. If a corpse was thought to be Confederate, they documented it, refilled the hole, and moved on. Although this was only a few months after the battle, Mother Nature had done her job and many bodies were unrecognizable. Identifying clothes and other possessions were often missing, either lost to pilfering or to animals. For some, underwear was the only remaining clue as to whether the skeleton in life had fought for the North or the South. The Union issued wool, a southern soldier usually wore cotton.

In 1864, "Elliott's Map of the Battlefield of Gettysburg Pennsylvania made from an accurate survey of the ground with transit and chain" was published. It included a keyed chart of the elements being documented—critical landmarks, the location of Union, Confederate and horse graves, some of the battlefield hospitals, and where well-known Generals died.

Elliott, an engineer from Philadelphia, probably did his research in the fall of 1863. It must have been after the decision to move the Union bodies to the National Cemetery and before Weaver and Biggs actually did it, because he included the layout plan for the National Cemetery on the map.

Aside from his own observations and measurements, Elliott used information from Dr. O'Neal, Samuel Weaver, local witnesses, and area farmers struggling to recover from the battle-inflicted damage to their properties. The included key shows Union graves marked with crosses, Confederate ones with vertical lines, and horses with commas.

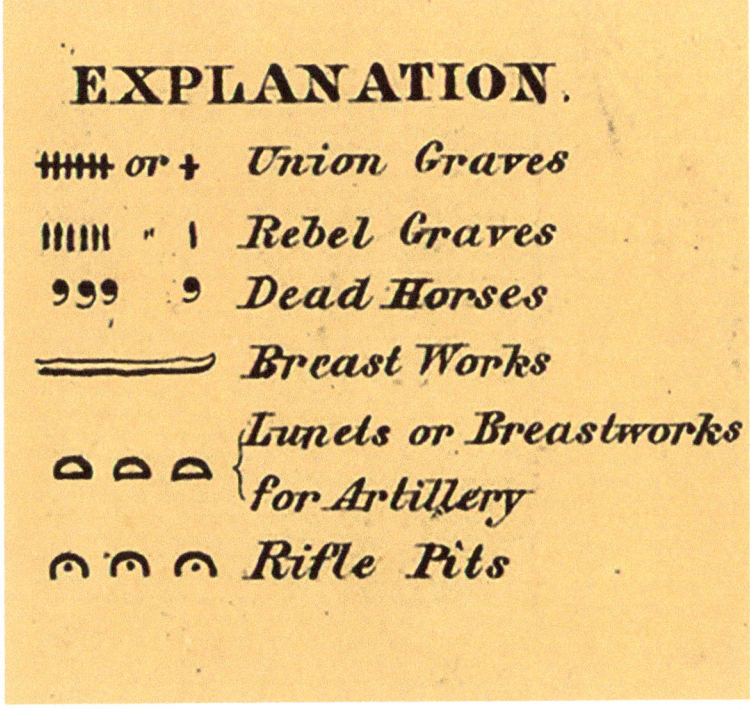

Codes used on Elliott's Map to identify graves

Having explored Gettysburg so many times, this map is especially shocking to me. It's one thing to know that almost 8000 people lost their lives in this small Pennsylvania farming town—it's quite another to be able to visualize exactly what that might look like. For example, the bottom right quarter of the Elliott map illustrates the carnage in and around Rose's Woods. Wandering around that peaceful patch of ground as historians describe the chaos of the second day certainly gave me a good idea of what had happened there—and certainly Timothy O'Sullivan's photograph of dead Confederate soldiers lying at the southwest edge of Rose's Woods (Page 84) is sobering. However, the sheer number of quantifying vertical hash marks representing lost human lives broke my heart anew—as did the handwritten labels, "500 rebel Graves just west of Rose Woods" and "400 Rebel Graves" indicated inside Rose Woods.

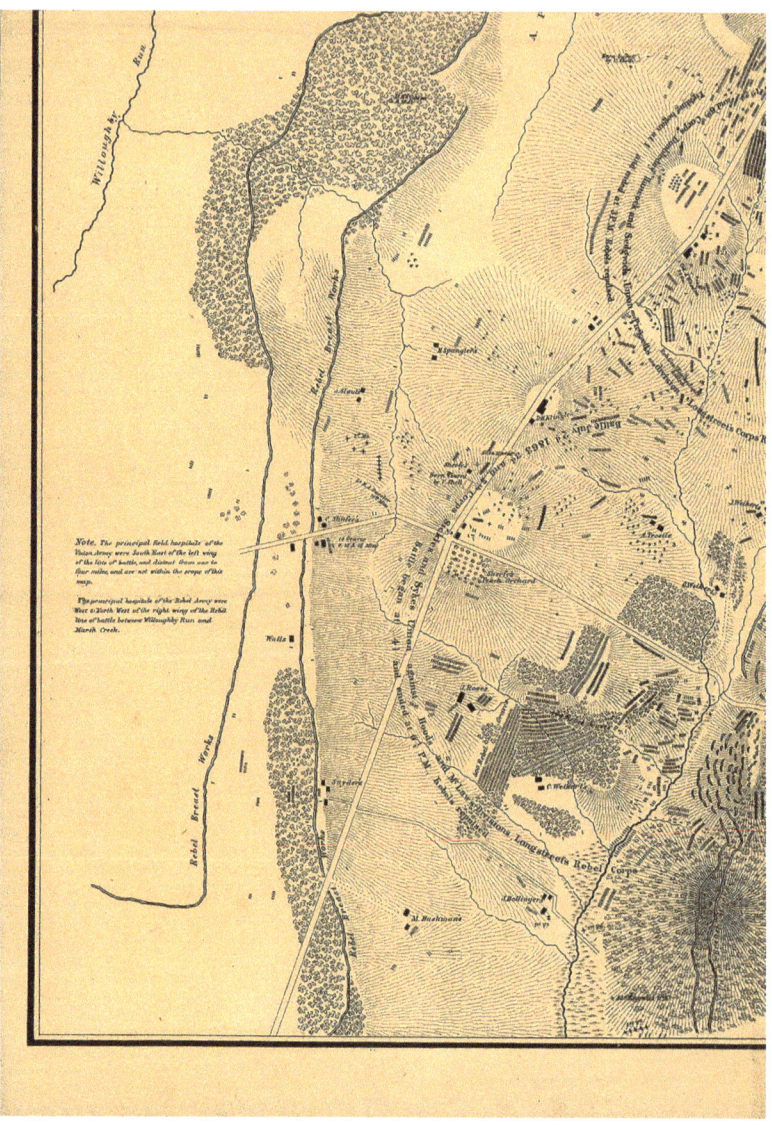

Bottom Left Quarter of Elliott's Map showing Rose's Farm.

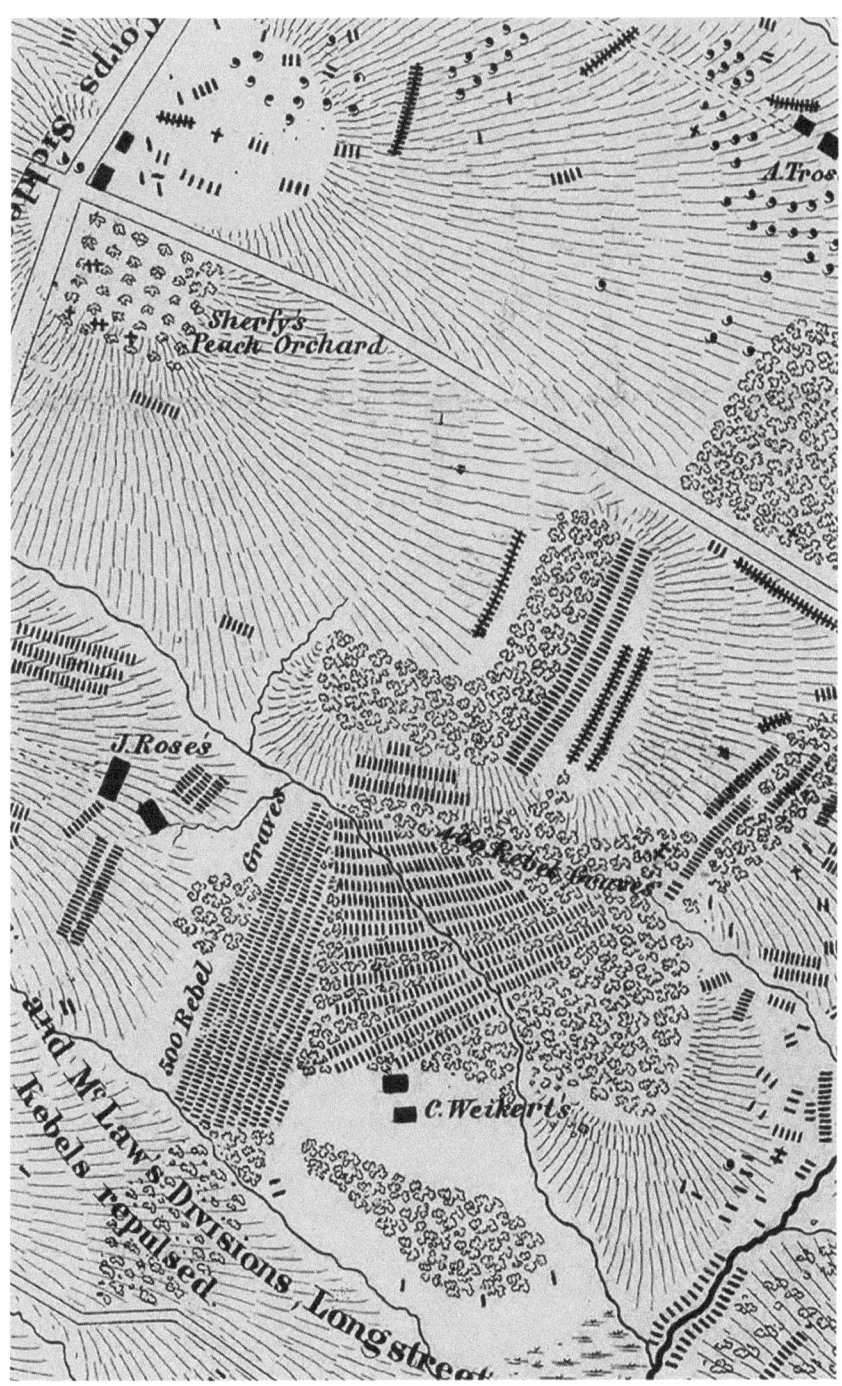

Detail of Rose Farm Confederate Burials as per Elliott's Map

MWSA Gettysburg Writers' Retreat

As I further examined the Elliott Map, another gruesome aspect of the cost of battle struck me. Commas. Lot's of them. Horses! Especially in the area around and behind the Angle and over the small hill sloping back to Meade's Head Quarters on Taneytown Road. (See the lower right hand quadrant of Elliott's Map below.)

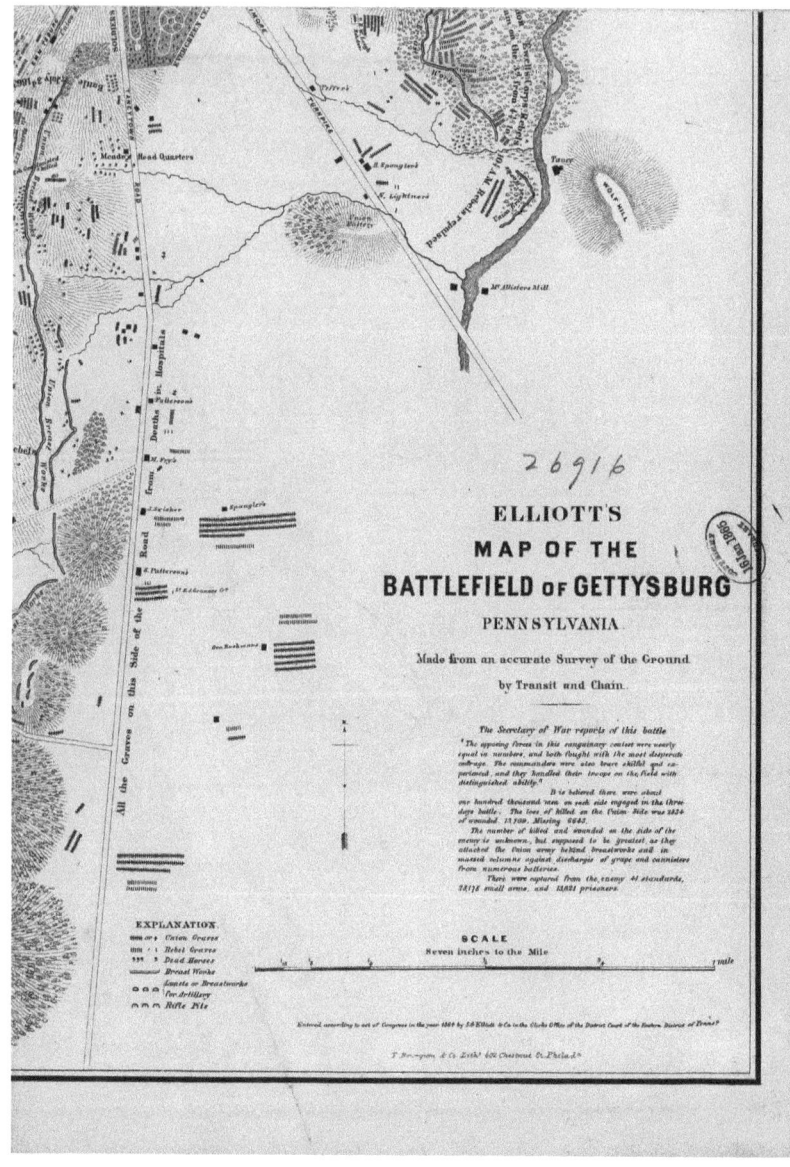

Lower right quadrant of Elliott's Map

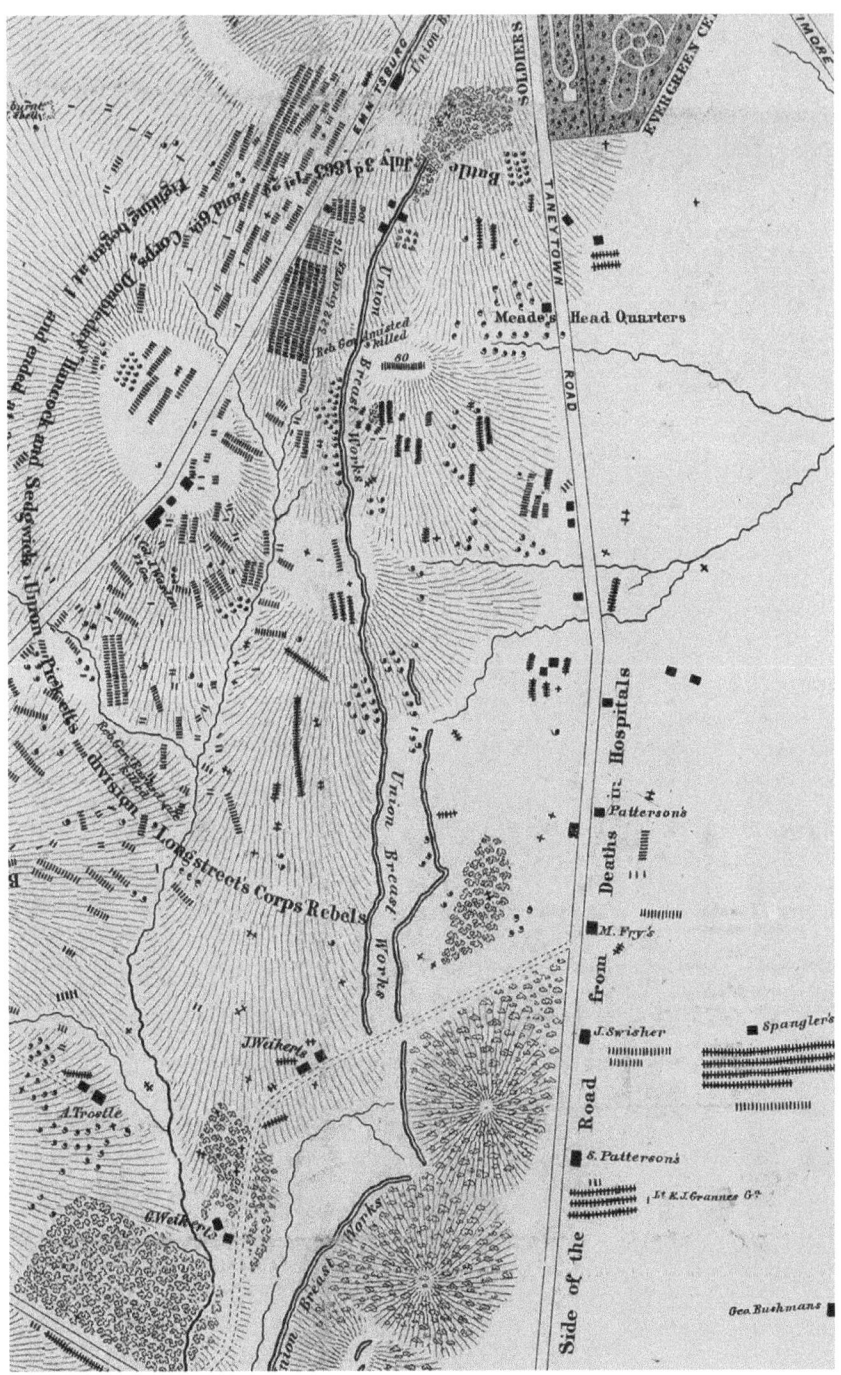

Details of the area around the location of "Pickett's Charge"

MWSA Gettysburg Writers' Retreat

Brady's photographers combined with Elliott's Map completes the dramatic tableau—especially, this picture of the Widow Leister's home which became Meade's Headquarters during the battle. The image of dead horses on the lawn and on the road are especially compelling when you consider the numbers indicated on the map.

The Leister House, photographed by Alexander Gardner on July 6, 1863.
(Library of Congress)

Although the Elliott Map is a good indicator of the magnitude of the tragedy—and a reflection of what witnesses at the time believed, over the years, it has been challenged by historians. Like anything associated with

Gettysburg, from Jenny Wade to the location of the O'Sullivan photo, "Harvest of Death," there are lots of opinions among Gettysburg residents, visitors, and reenactors.

Harvest of Death, photographed by Timothy O'Sullivan, of soldiers killed on the first day of battle in Gettyburg, July 1, 1863. (Library of Congress)

Some people dispute that there were as many "Rebs" buried in the Rose Woods as Elliott's Map shows. They have reviewed the units who fought nearby and determined that there just weren't that many men in them, dead or alive. Other folks argue that there are other errors of omission or commission. Of course, anything is possible. The Roses had considerable damage to their farming business because of the battle and it would have been to their advantage to present a larger claim to maximize government and insurance payments. Reporting that almost 1000 bodies were buried on your land would capture the attention of any assessor. It's also possible that Elliott made an honest mistake. Maybe he was told there were 50 bodies west of Rose's Woods and 40 buried in the woods. Maybe.

There are people who believe that those closest to a historical event in time and place are best qualified to say what happened and that their testimony is to be valued higher than other evidence. There are others who say that those who participated in some grand event are too close to appreciate the totality of it. One must step away and analyze such events from a distance.

Fine details are important when it comes to funding and when it came to getting those men home to their families in the years after the war. However, when you are riding a bus throughout the area trying to get a feel for what did happen, the Elliott Map is like a sweeping historical novel. It represents perceived heroes and villains entangled in a dramatic struggle for justice. There is pathos and horror, hatred and honor—and a picture of everlasting sorrow.

The final question is where are all of those bodies now? For the most part, the Union dead lie on Cemetery Hill in the National Cemetery. Current thinking has at least seven Confederates still buried with them by mistake. There are probably others lost forever in the grounds around Gettysburg. Over the years, the partial remains of nine bodies had been recovered, examined, and buried together in a vault. As late as 1996, a body believed to be a Mississippian was found near the railway cut where so many died on the first day of the battle. Now, Confederate or Union, these Americans were reburied in the same coffin with honors under an oak tree in the Gettysburg National Military Park.

The vast majority of the Confederate dead were sent south between 1872 and 1875, most at the behest of the Hollywood Ladies Memorial Association in Richmond Virginia. They contracted with Dr. Rufus Weaver, the son of Samuel Weaver to manage the process. Over three years, Rufus Weaver processed 3300 bodies. The majority of them are interred on Gettysburg Hill in the Hollywood Cemetery along the James River—in the shadow of a pyramid monument.

You can download a copy of Elliott's Map at the National Archives as well as the work of Brady's employees—specifically, photographers Timothy O'Sullivan and Alexander Gardner's images that are included in this essay.

MWSA Authors

Photo by Joyce Faulkner

Joyce Faulkner

Joyce Faulkner is an award-winning author, ghostwriter, and columnist. She is a previous President of MWSA, an avid reader and researcher, a book designer, and co-owner of Red Engine Press. She began writing in her early teens and received her first award for an essay she wrote about Jefferson Davis from the Arkansas Chapter of the Daughters of the Confederacy.

Her fictional works include: *Losing Patience*, *USERNAME*, *In the Shadow of Suribachi*, *Windshift*, and *Vala's Bed*. Nonfictional books with writing partner Pat McGrath Avery are: *Sunchon Tunnel Massacre Survivors*, *Role Call: Women's Voices*, and the Fun Days series of children's books. Along with Pat Avery, she has written for and/or designed several ongoing magazines and newspapers including MWSA's Dispatches, The Branson Bugle, The Iwo Jima Association of America's Black Sands Newsletter, TheCelebrityCafe.com, and Salute.

She holds a Bachelor of Science in Chemical Engineering from the University of Pittsburgh and a Masters of Business Administration from Cleveland State University and she studied writing at the University of Arkansas.

Photo by Joyce Faulkner

Photo by Pat McGrath Avery

TWO

Thoughts on a Common Soldier

Mindy Phillips Lawrence

Whose bones do I walk on?
Was he wearing blue or grey on the day he fell?
What were his thoughts as he hid in the trees,
filled with fear, before he gave his life for
what he believed?
His marker is a simple rock,
No place of origin carved there.
He never shared his name,
never found a way home.
This man, this solitary soldier,
marched into battle with the notion of
quick victory.
But here he is, pounded into the rubble of war,
not knowing whether he won or lost.

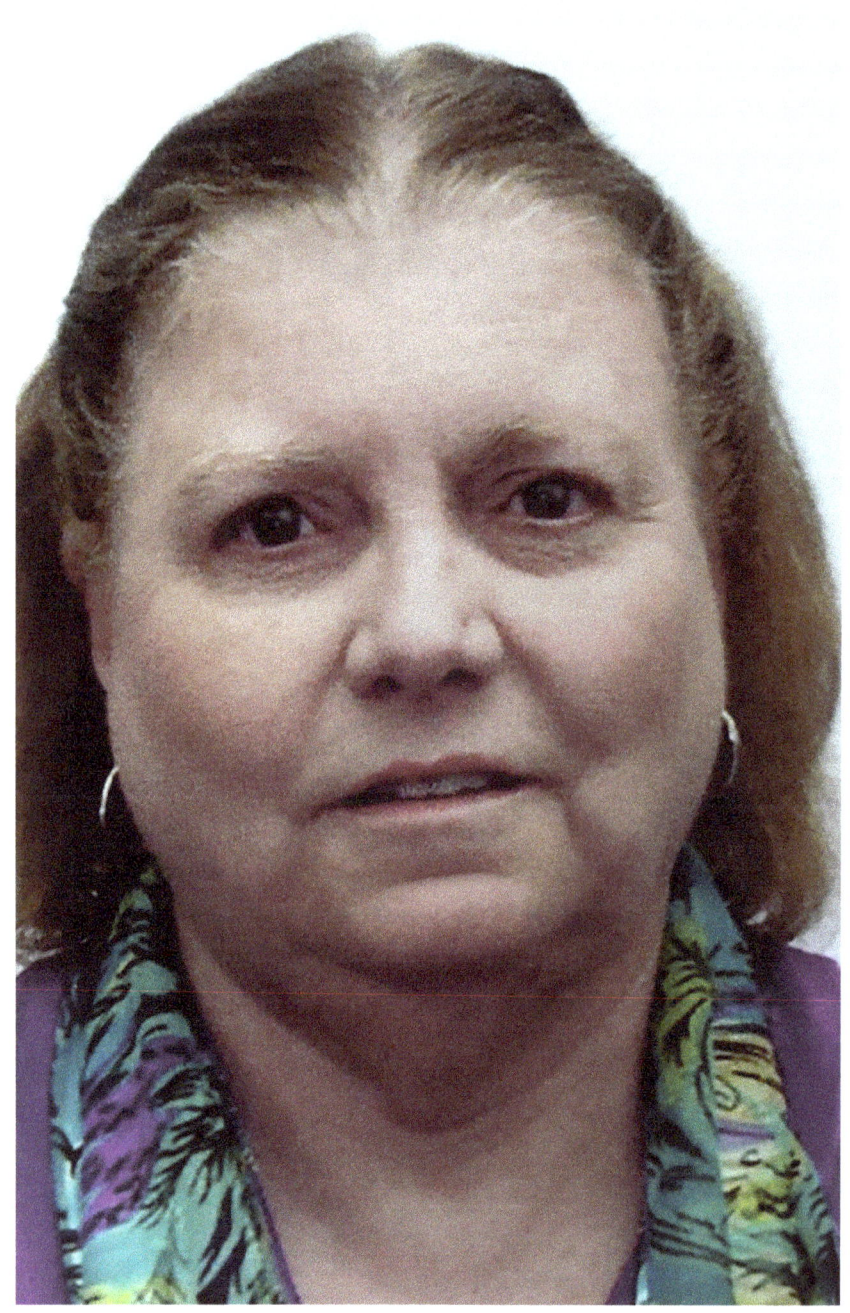

Mindy Phillips Lawrence

Mindy Phillips Lawrence is a writer, poet, and artist from Springfield, Missouri. She proofreads and writes the column An Itty-Bitty Column on Writing in Sharing with Writers newsletter founded by Carolyn Howard-Johnson. Lawrence is currently working on an e-book based on her posts from that column.

Mindy retired from working as a Workforce Development Specialist for the State of Missouri in March 2016 and continues to write, do calligraphy work, and make handmade Coptic-bond journals.

Photo by Pat McGrath Avery

Photo by Pat McGrath Avery

THREE

The Wait

Joe Epley

The fighting is over.

I'm leaning back against a rock wall. Don't know exactly how I got here. Bodies are all around me. Some moving, twitching, moaning. Others still, quiet, laying in piles of mixed blue and gray, all splotched with red and black blood.

A Yankee soldier is resting against the wall beside me. I ask if he is dead. "Don't know. I don't hurt. How 'bout you?"

"Don't think so, Ain't got no feelings, though. Did we fight each other?"

A gaping hole distorts his jaw.

"Must have if you were with them Rebs that charged into us," he says. "Where you from?"

"Lincoln County, I'm with the 52nd North Carolina Infantry."

"Lincoln County? You have a county down South named after ol' Abe?"

"Hell no! We were named after a Revolutionary War general. Although some folks want to change the name since Abe started this war."

"To these poor sods around us, it doesn't matter who started the war. Did you ever see such carnage?"

"No, sir. I was in a few skirmishes where people got killed and all, but nothing like this."

"When are they gonna help us?"

"Don't know. Guess we wait a while."

* * *

It is late in the day, much later than I remember. The sun is on the horizon. Last I remember is early afternoon. I'm marching across the fields with company G, most all of us Lincoln County boys. They call us the 'Dry Pond Dixies.' Ain't much of a name, but it's ours.

First Sergeant William Thompson urges us on even as men are falling around us. Young George Nixon walking beside me suddenly is not there anymore. Cannon balls burst among us, showering me in dirt and blood.

I'm nearly knocked down by the concussions. But we keep advancing... across the Emmitsburg Road ... on toward the wall of blue.

We get closer. Everybody yells and screams. Sergeant Thompson pulls a straggler to his feet and pushes him forward. He doesn't break stride. His face is grisly, his eyes fiery. He shouts to me, "What you waiting for? Keep the line straight!" He looks at me like I'm a slacker, but I ain't.

Individual Yankees now are in plain view along Cemetery Ridge, now within rifle range. More boys go down. Captain James Kincaid stops the company line; we aim, shoot. It is blistering hot, the thick smoke suffocating. The Sergeant gets us moving forward again.

Deafening noise comes from blasting rifles, booming cannon, painful screams, and thousands of yelling soldiers trying to bolster their courage and frighten the enemy. Somehow the booming voice of Sergeant Thompson penetrates all that din. I see the Yankee faces now. Their eyes are wide, mouths grim. They are as scared as I am, but as determined to kill me as I am to kill them.

We are running toward them. Thirty yards, twenty yards. A canister of shrapnel and grape blasts into the line to my left. It catches Sergeant Thompson and flings him over me. In an instant, he's gone. Nothing in front but Yankee bayonets. Then nothing till I wake up on the wall.

* * *

Looking around I see Yankee soldiers sorting through the bodies. I hear one cry, "Here's another 'un alive." Two sad looking men in Confederate butternut pick up the wounded man and carry him away on a stretcher.

I try to yell to them that I'm over here—two of us still waiting. I ask my Yankee friend why no one is hearing us. He's puzzled too. We wait.

* * *

It is dark. Lanterns dance like fireflies across the battlefield as searchers look for more survivors. They don't come close to us. I want to stand and shout but can't move. So I wait.

During the night, my companion is talking again. He says he is a railway clerk from Hartford, Connecticut. I tell him I'm a farmer.

"What do you farm in North Carolina?" he asks.

"We grow cotton, corn, and oats, mostly. Tobacco don't grow good in our county."

"You got slaves to work the fields?"

I laugh. "Nah. Can't afford one. Just me and my Pa."

"I thought all you Southerners had slaves?"

"Most of us don't. Mostly just the big plantation folks have slaves. Some of us don't want them. Cost too much to keep one up. Besides, ain't right owning somebody else. But my neighbor has a few, and Pa rents one now and then to help with the harvest."

"So you joined up to protect slavery?"

"No. Never thought about it. I joined cause you Yankees were going to invade North Carolina and I don't like that. I mean, I don't hate Yankees; just that old Abe wants to put his boot on our throats and that ain't right. How about you? Why did you join?"

"Patriotic thing to do, I guess. All my friends joined right after you folks fired on Fort Sumter. My wife wasn't too happy about it, her with a new baby and all. My unit has had it pretty easy until we got here."

We talk through the night. The lanterns don't return. We wait.

"How come you don't have shoes on?" he asks.

"Done wore out what I started the war with. Got me some shoes off a dead Yankee two days ago, but they pinched my feet, gave me blisters. I threw 'em away. Thought I might pick up a better pair from some unlucky bastard who don't need them anymore."

The sun is coming up behind us. My Yankee friend says "Did you know it's Independence Day—the 4th of July? Wonder if they will have fireworks to celebrate?"

"Didn't we have enough fireworks yesterday?

* * *

The sun is up for an hour, it's getting hot. Swarms of flies are buzzing around, feasting on the carcasses of men and horses scattered about me. No moans or whimpers resonate through the stillness. I see Joe Howard from my company locked with a Yankee corporal, both squeezing the other's throat.

We hear wagons and horses. They are collecting the dead.

Midday, the stench is terrible—feces, body rot, blood. I don't retch. Although it is stifling hot, I don't sweat. The harvest of bodies continue. The gatherers lift corpses and fling them onto a wagon bed. When the chariot of death is full, its two-horse team pulls it away. Another quickly takes its place, an endless procession in the grim task of gathering the trophies of battle.

* * *

It's been twenty-four hours since Colonel James K. Marshall orders our brigade of four North Carolina regiments forward on a mile long march across parched fields toward Cemetery Ridge south of Gettysburg. We are part of 15,000 man army under General James Longstreet making a dazzling mile-wide display of military might, though if you looked closely, the uniforms are drab, mismatched, dirty. The regimental flags and Stars and Bars add color, but they are limp, there is no breeze. Then as we move, the standard bearers wave the pennants from side to side. We all cheer.

The 52nd is a proud regiment. We march confidently because we are dumb enough to think we are invincible and after three days of struggle, the battle will be won. That is until we see the smoke puffs from nearly a hundred cannon a mile away. It's the start of the death rain.

A sharpshooter knocks Colonel Marshall from his saddle, putting a bullet in his right eye. He dies before hitting the ground. A hundred yards from the enemy lines, the 52nd's commander, Lieutenant Colonel Marshall Parks, is shot in both legs, putting him out of action. An artillery burst kills the regimental major. The bugles blow recall, only about half of General Longstreet's army return from the battlefield. The 52nd loses 464 men dead, wounded, captured, or missing, more than half of its soldiers who started that summer stroll known as Pickett's Charge.

*** * * ***

They pick up my companion and take him to the macabre cart. Nice chap. Hard to think of him as the enemy. I wait.

Two tired Yankees, bandannas covering their nose and mouth, pick me up and lug me to the same ghastly carriage. At least I don't weigh more than a sack of grain. They heave me over the side of the wagon, up on top of a stack of other soldiers who died for their cause. A blood-caked Yankee shoe is in my face.

After a short ride, they unload us from the wagon. We are separated from the blue coats. The Union boys are laid out on the ground in neat lines as sergeants and officers with notebooks try to identify who is who and collect watches and wallets. A team of Confederate prisoners strips shoes, belts, holsters, swords, canteens and other accouterments from the Union dead and throw the items into piles for issue to new recruits.

Not as much fuss is made over us Confederates. We are thrown in a pile away from the enemy dead. I wonder when they will sort us. Another wait. Glad I pinned my pa's name and address under my shirt this morning.

MWSA Authors

Photo by Pat McGrath Avery

Joe Epley

Joe Epley has worn many hats over his adult life—public relations executive, Green Beret, television journalist, change agent and novelist. He has canoed Arctic wilderness rivers, hiked the Australian outback, helped restore homes destroyed by hurricanes, and provided guidance for the introduction of the public relations profession to Russia and the old Soviet Union.

Epley founded and served 38 years as CEO of Epley Associates, a Charlotte based public relations firm with a global practice. He also founded and for two years was the global chair of the Worldcom Public Relations Group, the world's largest consortium of independent public relations firms with offices in 35 countries. A past national head of the Public Relations Society of America, the PRSA Foundation, the PRSA College of Fellows and the Counselor's Academy, his skills and leadership in the profession earned him international recognition and numerous honors including PRSA's prestigious Gold Anvil for life time achievements.

Long active in civic affairs, he served on the boards of directors of the Charlotte Chamber of Commerce, North Carolina Citizens for Business and Industry (now the North Carolina state chamber of commerce), the Blue Ridge Parkway Foundation and Charlotte's World Affairs Council. He is a long time board member of The Marketing Alliance, a publicly traded company with operations in the insurance, construction and entertainment industries.

Epley is a member of the Halls of Fame at the University of North Carolina School of Journalism and the Defense Information School. His successes earned him North Carolina's prestigious "Order of the Long Leaf Pine" award for citizens who have made significant contributions to the state in business, arts, education, or public service.

His newest novel, *A Passel of Trouble*, was published in October 2016. His first novel, *A Passel of Hate*, was awarded a Silver Medal from the Military Writers Society of America and named an Editor's Choice by the Historical Novel Society.

Photo by Pat McGrath Avery

FOUR

I Will Not Be a Number

By Richard Davidson

Rain, mud, and blood marked the takeover of the Spangler farm on Blacksmith Shop Road in Gettysburg, Pennsylvania on July 1, 1863 as the battling Union and Confederate forces surging back and forth left many mangled bodies in their wake. George Spangler's farm became the main battlefield hospital, although every farm quartered some of the wounded. During the course of the three-day Battle of Gettysburg, more than 1800 Union soldiers and 100 Confederates would be treated at the Spangler Farm. Because of heavy rains the basements of those buildings that had them were flooded. Many of the wounded faced treatment and operations under the eaves of the Spangler's massive barn, with rainwater splashing them as it cascaded from the roof. Seven Union surgeons under the direction of Dr. Daniel G. Brinton of Chester, Pennsylvania tried desperately to keep up with the incoming wounded. Most serious wounds in limbs led to amputations using the same tools and cloths on multiple patients without any form of sanitization. Those with major head and body trauma were deemed mortally wounded and given only pain-killer treatments to ease their inevitable transition to death. This is the story of one such patient.

* * *

We look in on him inside the barn on July 2nd, one day after he was shot during the first round of fighting. Doctors and assistants rush back and forth, trying to cope with the chaos around them. Our subject, an officer, talks with a private he has had brought to his bedside following that enlisted man's lower leg amputation.

Danforth, I've discovered an intriguing aspect of this process of dying; and the surgeon assures me that I have no hope of eluding death. My epiphany is that I am now living in the past, present and future, all at the same time. To be precise, I am in quite present agony because of the minié ball that pierced my left side and shattered to slice up my bowels. The doctor managed to clamp off the bleeding, but I'm oozing other fluids into my gut and none of my internal plumbing works anymore. I'm living in the past, because I actually am seeing various periods of my life as I prepare for death and I'm wondering how a Confederate soldier could have shot me in the left side as I stood behind the center of our ranks urging the men forward during the very first volley of this battle. One of our own men must have shot me, either accidentally or on purpose. The how and why don't really matter at this point. I'm afraid that in death I'll have a kinship with that graycoat, Stonewall Jackson, who was also shot by his own people at Chancellorsville a couple of months ago. He held off death for eight days. I doubt that I'll last that long. The battle here at Gettysburg is still raging, and I don't expect to outlive its hostilities by more than a day or two.

"Hey, Doc, it hurts pretty badly. Could you conjure up another one of those opium pills? ... Better make it two. Thanks."

Getting back to my living in other times, I feel like I'm in the future, because even though I'm closed up here in Spangler's barn, my mind sees acres of bodies of men and horses and gravestones. They're going to write books about the thousands on both sides who died here at Gettysburg, and I refuse to be one of their anonymous numbers. I'm drafting you to document that I've had a good life, Private Danforth. Your job will be to tell my story to others so that I won't be completely forgotten. I reckon that the closest thing people have to life after death is someone remembering them.

Yes, I realize that you have your own wound to worry about, but you'll get over that amputation below your left knee. They'll give you a wooden leg, and you'll go back to civilian life. I wish you the very best of futures. I'm picking on you to be the keeper of my memories because I've seen you writing long letters home. That tells me that you know how to handle the language and that you have caring people to share stories with. Both of those things suit my goals and portend a thriving life for you. Don't get me wrong; I'll see that you're paid for passing along my story. My brother Charlie is here with the Wisconsin Sharpshooters, and I'll ask him to take care of your needs.

As I said earlier, people are going to think of those dying here at Gettysburg as faceless numbers. You're going to remind them that I was a human being with a damned interesting life. Here we go; you should start writing now.

My full name is George Henry Stevens, although I'm known to most as George H. Stevens. I doubt that many know my middle name ... I'll try not to ramble so much. Between the pain and those pills, it's a little hard to think straight.

I guess I was one of the lucky ones, being born into a family of some means in New York City and later educated in private schools there. My birth date was December 8, 1831, just about thirty-one-and-a-half years ago. My parents were socially active, due to my father, John, being a shipping merchant. He and my mother, Lucy, were well regarded, both for their personalities and for Dad's ability to import hard-to-obtain commodities for the upper class folks. I was the fourth of five children and the only one who left New York looking for adventure and opportunity at an early age. Actually, my adventures started in New York City, following the Astor Place riot in 1849. I joined the 7th Regiment of the National Guard after seeing how well the militia handled the angry mob. Their acts of courage convinced me that there was something special about a military life, at least for a while. Without additional riots to put down, I became bored as a member of the Guard, and in 1852, at twenty-one years of age, I drew upon my father's shipping connections to secure a passage to Australia. I had always considered that a special place with great challenges and opportunities for young people.

Unfortunately, the real Australia didn't match my fantasies. Most of the country was completely undeveloped, and there were far too few women to satisfy the number of men there. I tried several business ventures in Australia, but none of them worked out. Romances didn't either. I finally gave up and returned to the States and New York in the summer of 1855. Fortunately, my old friends and contacts pointed me toward an opportunity in Milwaukee, going into the retail business with a local man named V. V. Livingston.

"Hey, Doc, that pill's wearing off. Get me another one when you get a chance."

As I was saying, I ended up working a business in Milwaukee, and in my spare time I took another crack at the military by joining the Second Company Light Guard. It was more of a fraternal group than a regiment, and I won a prize medal as the best drilled member. I was a sergeant then. The combination of military and merchant work led me to move to Fox Lake, Wisconsin in the fall of 1858, where I opened a grocery store and sent for my brother Charlie to help me run it.

"Double thanks, Doc; I won't take the second pill until I really need it. I have to keep my head clear while I tell Danforth my story. He's a good listener and writes well too."

Things get slow in Fox Lake during the winter months, so I organized a voluntary military unit I called the Citizens Guard. It kept me interested in something beyond business. ... I shouldn't say that. I was involved at the Congregational Church, even though my parents had raised me Episcopalian. Through church contacts, I met Harriet Purdy and married her in 1859 on March 23rd. If she were here, she'd be pleased that I remember our wedding date.

Harriet and I had some good times together, despite the separations caused by my military obligations and the war. Our son Walter was born in February of 1860, and she's carrying a second child right now. I won't be around for him or her, but I hope Harriet raises that child to think well of me. You'll have to greet him or her for me, Danforth. I hope you can be like a godfather to my kids.

Anyway, in April of 1861, when President Lincoln called for more troops to put down the rebellion, they gave me a commission as a captain and instructed me to reorganize my Citizens Guard unit and recruit more men for it. We met our requirement right away and marched to Camp Randall in Madison. There, we were renamed Company "A" of the Second Regiment Wisconsin Volunteer Infantry, and were the first unit to change our enlistment from three months to three years. They transported our regiment to Washington, D.C., and we saw our first action at the First Battle of Bull Run.

Following Bull Run, there were a whole string of battles, some with the 2nd Wisconsin acting alone, and later as part of the Iron Brigade, which included the 2nd, 6th, and 7th Wisconsin regiments plus regiments from Indiana and Michigan. At Second Bull Run, I ended up in command of the 2nd Wisconsin as a captain because of the loss of the colonel and the wounding of the lieutenant colonel. I missed the Antietam battle because of illness. – There was so much of that among the troops everywhere. I was a major, serving under Burnside at Fredericksburg, and a lieutenant colonel under Hooker at the Second Battle of Fredericksburg. We had a major skirmish with the enemy at Fitz-Hugh Crossing just prior to the Chancellorsville combat, but we weren't involved in the main event there.

"Hold it for a minute, Danforth, while I take my reserve opium pill."

"You've been through so much, sir. I didn't join the Second Wisconsin until just after Second Fredericksburg. I was with you at that skirmish before Chancellorsville, and then got hit with you yesterday."

Yes, yesterday was the capper, in several ways. You're done with soldiering and will go home to be with your family. I'm on my way out and will go home to God. I'll soon find out what He thinks of soldiers and our killing each other…. I started to say old soldiers, but I won't live to see my thirty-second birthday. The worst damn thing about yesterday isn't that we got hit during the first full-scale volley of this battle, but that the 2nd Wisconsin lost so many men. Doc told me that only 34 men were present for roll call on Cemetery Hill last night. We started the day with 306 men, 278 of whom were combatants. That's the number that fought in the morning to keep the Confederates, under Archer, from breaking through from McPherson Ridge to the heights on Cemetery Hill. We held them back, but due to the way we recruit units made up of neighbors, there are going to be many villages in Wisconsin without any young men left.

Believe it or not, Danforth, you're one of the lucky ones. These surgeons and self-trained medical people can save those wounded in their limbs through amputations, but a snowball in hell has a better chance of surviving than those of us who were hit in the head or the gut. Then there are all those who die from diseases before the battles even start. I wonder if men on the two sides of this war will ever be friends again…. God, this gut of mine hurts. The pills don't nearly free me from pain.

"I've taken seven pages of notes, sir. I think that's enough for now. You try to rest. As soon as there's a lull in the fighting, I'll send one of the assistants here to fetch your brother, Charlie. Sharpshooters don't fight after the sun sets, not that there is much sun getting through the battle smoke and frequent rainstorms. We'll get him here in time. I promise."

* * *

Lieutenant Colonel George H. Stevens succumbed on July 5, 1863, two days after the fighting at Gettysburg ceased. His remains were buried at Evergreen Cemetery in Gettysburg, with his family stating that they planned to take him back to Wisconsin after the war ended. Thanks to the dedication of a new National Cemetery adjacent to Evergreen on November 19, 1863, marked by Lincoln's Gettysburg Address, the Stevens family decided that he should permanently rest there. He is buried in a grave immediately behind and to the left of a large marker that reads WISCONSIN 73 BODIES.

Death did not end the story of George H. Stevens. At the Iron Brigade Reunion in 1887, a Clark County veteran said in an interview, "The first captain of Company A was George H. Stevens. He was killed as lieutenant colonel at the battle of Gettysburg. He was a splendid soldier (the only soldier so described)." Excerpting from Reminiscences of the Battle of Gettysburg by First Lieutenant Cornelius Wheeler, U.S.V. [Read April 5, 1893.]: Wheeler quotes Mr. H. J. Fahnestock, at that time a resident of Gettysburg, from his letter to Wheeler, "There is no question that the opening fight was between the two roads (the Fairfield and Chambersburg pikes) and spread later in the fight to the north, beyond the Chambersburg pike. The spot where [General] Reynolds is reported to have received his death-wound was at a copse of trees almost due west from the main seminary building, and about equidistant between the Fairfield road and the Chambersburg pike." Wheeler goes on to summarize, "This is where the Iron Brigade, the Second Wisconsin in advance, opened the battle of Gettysburg. [It is also where George H. Stevens received his mortal wound shortly after 10:30 a.m. on the morning of July 1, 1863.]"

From Legend and Lore: Congregational Church, Fox Lake, WI, "In the opening volley on the first day of the Battle of Gettysburg, Captain (sic) George Stevens was killed. Just a short stone toss away from him, Lucius Fairchild, future governor of Wisconsin, lost his arm. George Stevens was buried at Gettysburg, and his wife Harriet is buried in Riverside Cemetery here. After the war, Fox Lake veterans organized George H. Stevens Post 100 of the Grand Army of the Republic. Harriet Stevens presented a beautiful silk banner to them." (on May 18, 1886)

Harriet had paid fifty dollars to have the banner made for the George H. Stevens GAR Post No. 100. In 1930, the GAR was disbanded, and the banner was given to Lucy Hunter, the adult daughter of George Stevens. She had not yet been born when he died. Lucy decided to give the banner to the Fox Lake Public Library, where it was in a display case until the library moved to a new building in 1951. During the move someone at the library decided to discard the old GAR banner. A local veteran, Bill Linke, saw the banner on the garbage truck and rescued it. After an intervening period, Bill donated the banner to the Fox Lake American Legion Post. They held the banner in gradually declining condition until 1990, when they decided to raise funds to restore it as a valuable piece of history. The fundraising was completed in 2001 after some extra special events to achieve the necessary goal, and the restored banner was returned to Fox Lake, Wisconsin on Memorial Day in 2002. It was dedicated and enshrined in the American Legion Post during the 2002 Fox Lake Historical Days celebration. Harriet's original cost for the banner had been $50. The cost for restoring it was $4595, and the display case for it cost $1475.

George H. Stevens: adventurer, businessman, and splendid soldier, achieved his goal. He lives on in the traditions of Fox Lake, Wisconsin. He is not an anonymous number in the statistics of Gettysburg.

George Henry Stevens
Lieutenant Colonel, Second Minnesota Infantry

Richard Davidson

Richard Davidson is the author of the self-help guidebook: *DECISION TIME! Better Decisions for a Better Life*. He has written the five-novel Lord's Prayer Mystery Series: *Lead Us Not into Temptation, Give Us this Day our Daily Bread, Forgive Us Our Trespasses, Thy Will Be Done*, and *Deliver Us from Evil*. He is the editor of an anthology, *Overcoming: An Anthology by the Writers of* OCWW. His latest three novels, *Implications, Impulses*, and *Impostor* from his new Imp Mysteries series, continue to chronicle the exploits of Arthur Blake and the investigative associates who aided him in the earlier series, taking their interests in new directions. His current novel project is *Impending*, a historical novel tracing a family's history in the aftermath of the Battle of Gettysburg.

Mr. Davidson is Past President of Off-Campus Writers' Workshop, the oldest ongoing group of its kind in the U.S. and is the founder of the ReadWorthy Books Book Review Blog and the Independent Mystery Publishing Society (IMPS). Mr. Davidson is a Certified Lay Servant Speaker and a former Lay Leader in the United Methodist Church. He is also an aeronautical & astronautical engineer and a businessman.

Photo by Pat McGrath Avery

FIVE

The Sixth Copy

Florence March
October 28, 2016

Joy, Matt, Emily, and James knew they only had twenty minutes before total darkness settled over the hay field behind them. They knew because their aunt had told them they had to be inside before 6:00 PM this Tuesday evening, February 11, 2009.

They also knew because the warm glow of sunset had already marched across the sky from east to west, leaving behind a trail of inky black clouds and a sheet of darkness. Only one scrappy cloud still glowed red over the spot where the sun had sunk behind South Mountain. A chilly wind blew down off the frosty hills. The children shivered.

"Hurry up, everybody!" Joy urged. "Let's start by forming a circle.

Hold hands everyone. Close your eyes. Now repeat after me: In darkest night, in wind, and rain, Bring Abraham Lincoln back again."

"In darkest night, in wind, and rain," the children repeated. "Bring Abraham Lincoln back again."

"Now we're going to make a power ring," Joy said. "I'm going to squeeze your hand, Matt. Then Matt, squeeze Emily's hand, and Emily, pass the squeeze on around the circle to James. When it gets back to me, I'm going to pass it around again. Only the second time, pass it faster. Keep going faster and faster—squeeze and pass, squeeze and pass—until we feel the circle break apart. Then run into the parlor. Everyone understand? Okay. Get the circle ready. Are you all set? Go!"

"Squeeze, squeeze, squeeze, squeeze, squeeze," chanted the children.

"Squeeze, squeeze, squeeze, squeeze,squeeze, squeeze, squeeze, squeeze, squeeze, squeeze, squeeze, squeeze, squeeze, squeeze, squeeze, squeeze, run!"

A jumble of children crashed into the parlor, slamming the door behind them. James tripped over the cat, landing in a giggling pile on the rug. The other children tumbled down next to him, laughing to silliness.

And then to stillness as a black shadow loomed in the corner.

"Auntie, you nearly scared us to death!" Joy's sides were still heaving with exertion and excitement.

"Sorry. I was staying out of your way. Did you see Lincoln?"

"I knew we wouldn't see Lincoln." James was the family skeptic. "It's not even his birthday until tomorrow!"

"James, if you close your mind like that, you won't see anything. It's too late to do anything about it tonight, so come on into the kitchen. I've made you some hot chicken pot pie. You children need to warm up.

"But before we eat, I have something to give you. I want you to try again tomorrow night. I'm going to give you each a shiny new penny. Keep it with you."

"Auntie, what good is a penny? You can't buy anything with just one cent."

"This isn't just one cent. Look at it carefully. What do you see?"

Joy stared into her hand. "I see a bust of Abraham Lincoln."

"That's right. The Lincoln image on that penny was sculpted by the artist Victor David Brenner to celebrate Lincoln's 100th birthday. Brenner based this bas relief on a photograph taken by Mathew Brady. And 2009 is the 200th birthday of President Abraham Lincoln and the 100th birthday of the Lincoln penny. I believe that your pennies will help you channel the spirit of Abraham Lincoln," Auntie said. "Now let's have supper. I predict that things will be much different tomorrow night."

But Wednesday February 12, it rained. At 5:41 PM on Lincoln's birthday, the children were warm and dry in the parlor with their noses pressed against the cold, damp window, staring out into the dark as the rain pelted against the glass.

On Thursday, they were ready. At 5:35 PM, the children gathered on the soggy cold lawn. Pink clouds streaked the sky as the red-orange disk of the sun slowly sank behind the deep blue mountain range.

"Are we all ready?" Joy was their leader.

"Right!"

"Right!"

"Yes sirree, Bob! . . . .I think." James looked at her sideways. "We already missed Lincoln's birthday yesterday because it rained."

"James, we need you on board! Now, before we begin, let's make sure we all agree." Joy glared at James as a gust of freezing air stung her cheeks.

"One! There are five known copies of the Gettysburg Address."

"Right!"

"Two! We think Lincoln started with a scratch copy and handed it to his valet William H. Johnson, who traveled with Lincoln to Gettysburg."

"Right!"

"Three. We don't know what happened to that copy."

"Right!"

"Four. The only person who knows where the scratch copy is is Lincoln himself."

"And," broke in Matt, "Lincoln's dead! That's why we are going to contact his spirit. We are going to ask him what happened to the sixth copy." Matt was on-board with the project.

"And the best time to break through to the spirit world is at the moment that night fully cloaks the sky, the boundary between day and night." Emily was on-board too.

"James, so what are we going to do?"

"We are going to invoke Lincoln's spirit by chanting three times. Then we are going to form a power ring to open a portal to allow Lincoln's spirit to enter our world. When the ring breaks, we are going to run into the parlor. But I don't get it. Why do we need to run into the parlor?"

"Think about it. Where would you expect to find Lincoln? Inside reading a book by the fire, of course!"

"Then why aren't we doing this inside?"

"Because if we were inside, we couldn't see the moment the sky turned black, silly!"

"I get it!" Now James was on board. The team was ready. The last speck of sunlight flickered out behind the mountain.

"Okay everyone. Form a circle. Do you all have your pennies? Hold hands. Here we go!"

In darkest night, in wind, and rain,
Bring Abraham Lincoln back again.
In darkest night, in wind, and rain,
Bring Abraham Lincoln back again.
In darkest night, in wind, and rain,
Bring Abraham Lincoln back again.
Squeeze, squeeze, squeeze, squeeze,
squeeze, squeeze, squeeze, squeeze,
squeeze, squeeze, squeeze, squeeze,
squeeze, squeeze, squeeze, squeeze,
squeeze, squeeze, squeeze, squeeze, run!

The parlor door slammed behind them. A chilled wind whipped down the chimney and blasted against their faces, stopping them cold. The flames in the fireplace vanished. As the children stared at the glowing red coals, a single black wisp of smoke leisurely wound into the dark parlor. Before their eyes, the smoke transformed into a large black dog with a blue piece of paper in his mouth. The dog stared into Joy's eyes.

With a trembling hand, Joy reached out and took the paper. The paper was so light that it felt like nothing at all.

She pulled the paper close and began to read,

"Four score and seven years ago our fathers brought forth on this continent, a new nation, conceived in Liberty, and dedicated to the proposition that all men are created equal."

The shaking spread to her knees.

"Now we are engaged in a great civil war, testing whether that nation, or any nation, so conceived and so dedicated, can long endure."

"Let me see that." Matt's hand shot toward the paper.

At that same moment, in one smooth motion, the dog snatched the paper and lunged into the fireplace, vanishing in a puff of smoke.

Auntie stepped into the parlor from the kitchen. The fire was back. The room was warm. The flickering flames from the fireplace cast a cozy glow over the children. It looked like nothing had happened at all.

Joy was still shaking. So was Matt. James and Emily were huddled under a blanket on the sofa.

"Auntie, I had the Sixth Copy. I held it in my hand. But how can I know if Lincoln really sent me that copy from the spirit world, or if I just imagined it?"

"Joy, logic isn't going to help. Somewhere deep inside you, you know the answer."

"I do know the answer," Joy whispered. "There was a Sixth Copy. It doesn't exist anymore. That's the answer."

"I think you are right, but how will you prove it?" asked James.

"You can't." Auntie mused. " You can touch the spirit world, but you can't keep it. It doesn't belong here. And that's a good thing. It means it is not your time."

Joy shivered. Auntie gave her a hug. Joy melted into her lap.

"Auntie, I held the Sixth Copy. I had it in my hand. I know I did. I just know."

Living in the Shadow of the Ghost of the Confederate Flag

A song by Florence March

Living in the Shadow of the Ghost of the Confederate Flag
Living in the Shadow of the Ghost of the Confederate Flag

The ghost's the myth of the Lost Cause,
The shame of Jim Crow laws,
White hoods and white washed lies,
The ghost is tangled in our lives.

Are you really proud
That lynching was allowed?
Are you a rebel at the core?
The ghost is knocking at your door!

Living in the Shadow of the Ghost of the Confederate Flag
Living in the Shadow of the Ghost of the Confederate Flag

When you see that banner wave,
Know the ghost flies from his grave.
The ghost's a virus going 'round
With every flag you won't take down!

Put the flag to bed.
The Confederacy is dead!
Let our country heal.
Know the ghost is real!

Living in the Shadow of the Ghost of the Confederate Flag
Living in the Shadow of the Ghost of the Confederate Flag

The ghost lives on and on.
In privileged rights and deadly wrongs.
There's nothing civil about a war
Time to forgive, stop keeping score.

Open hearts and open minds.
Step into modern times.
Stop living in the past.
Unite America at last.

Stop living in the Shadow of the Ghost of the Confederate Flag
Stop living in the Shadow of the Ghost.

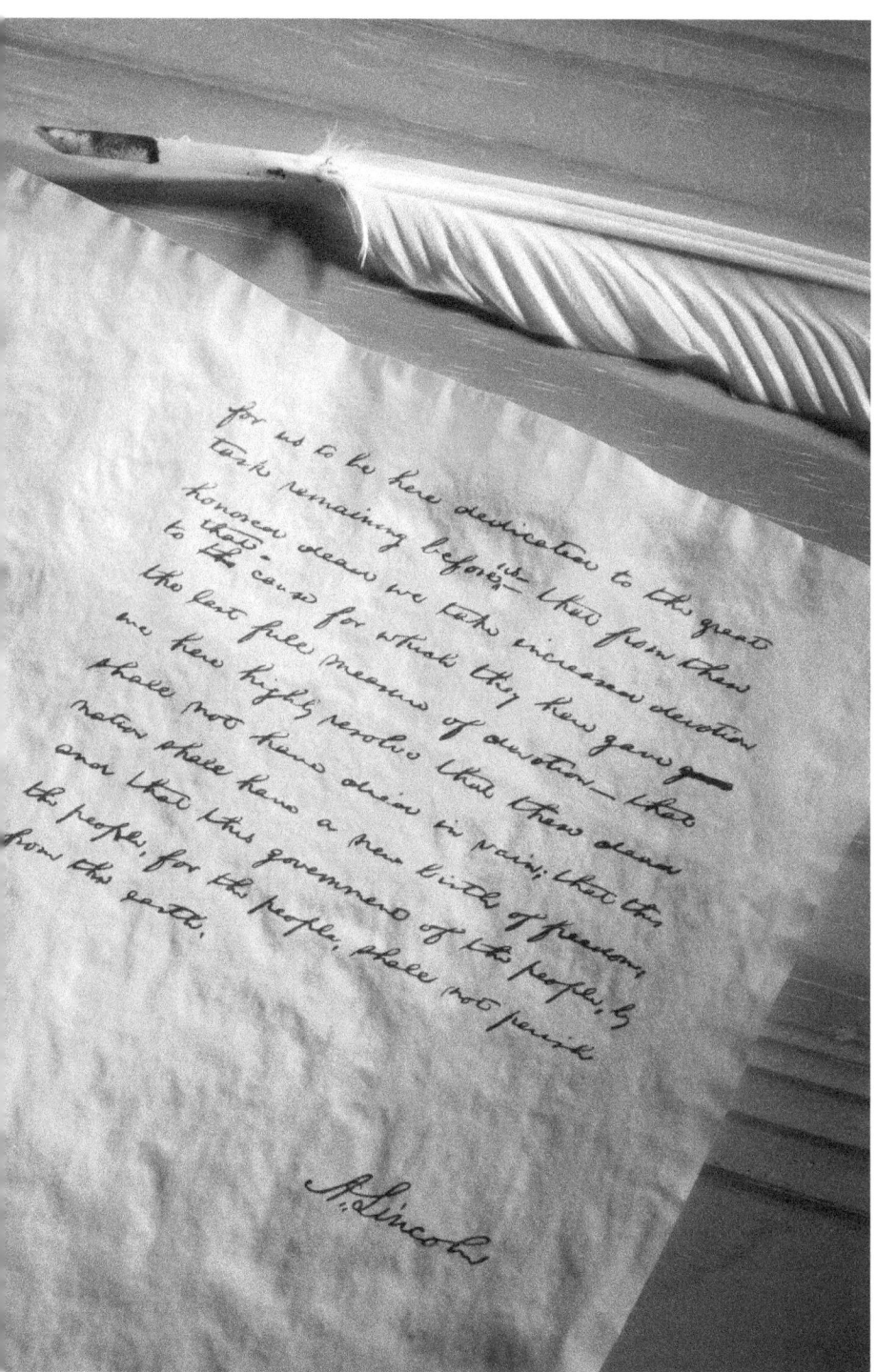

Florence March

Florence March is a song writer and storyteller from Gettysburg, Pennsylvania. Her song lyrics often address current social issues including songs such as "Women are Weavers" about women's leadership issues, "Midas Turned His Child To Gold" about protecting natural resources, and "Making Bigger Circles" about inclusivity. She owns Gettysburg Battlefield Bed & Breakfast on a Civil War farm on the Gettysburg Battlefield where she loves to organize history themed events for guests. She lives in Gettysburg with her wife Deborah March.

Photo by Pat McGrath Avery

Photo by Pat McGrath Avery

SIX

Reunion

Carolyn Schriber

Gettysburg, Pennsylvania
July 1-3, 1913

Becca Grenville's train ride to Gettysburg proved uneventful. Tom had provided a first-class ticket, so she was separated from the cars packed with the returning veterans. She was aware of them, of course. At every stop, new bands of men pushed their way aboard, all of them showing the ravages of old age but as eager as schoolboys for the trip. The track itself was sometimes bumpy and the sway of the carriage disorienting, but the scenery was beautiful. Becca found that she could relax once the train was underway. All the decisions had been made. Now control of the journey was out of her hands, and she found that oddly comforting. With nothing to think about for several hours, she closed her eyes and let happy memories wash over her.

The conductor approached her as the train slowed outside of Gettysburg. "We're stopping here at a special platform built to accommodate the veterans arriving at their campsites. You'll see the sea of tents they have provided for them. But you just stay seated. We'll go on into the main station once the men have been unloaded."

Becca stared out her window, almost unable to take in the scene unfolding before her. For as far as she could see in any direction, the ground was covered in orderly rows of long white tents, each large enough to hold ten or twelve men. Above many of them fluttered ragged battle flags. The platform and the surrounding paths swarmed with old men, many of them sporting their former uniforms. All along the platform, men were welcoming each other with bear hugs and handshakes, even if they wore opposing uniforms. Somewhere in the distance, she could hear the blare of trumpets and the steady beating of drums. Smoke curled lazily above the campfires being tended amidst the tents. And everywhere, there was an almost palpable air of excitement. Without fully realizing what she was doing, Becca grinned with delight at each small reunion she witnessed.

So it was with an easy heart that she stepped off the train in Gettysburg itself, ready now to face whatever surprises the town and its celebrations might have in store. A short one-block walk from the station brought her to the Gettysburg Hotel, an imposing four-story structure on the town square. The desk clerk had a frazzled look about him, as customers clamored for room keys, sought information on meal times, and asked directions to various battle sites. But he brightened when she gave him her name.

"Miss Rebecca Grenville? Oh, yes, you're Mr. Maloney's aunt, I understand. He's one of our owners, and he's asked that we take very good care of you."

"Oh, no—" she started to say. Tom Maloney was not her nephew, as least not yet, since he was showing no urgency about marrying her niece Gloria. Then she realized that instead of correcting the statement, she ought to be flattered and grateful for the care that had prepared a way for her. Smiling, she amended her words to say, "Thank you. I'm sure I will enjoy my stay."

"He also left a message for you. He'll be joining you for breakfast in the morning. We've reserved a lovely first-floor room for you. George, here, will take your bag and show you the way."

The young porter directed her across the lobby sitting area to an ornate door with a small brass number on it. "This is your room, ma'am." He held the door to let her step inside ahead of him. He carefully placed her satchel on the quilted counterpane that covered the iron bedstead. "There's a washroom attached right over here," he explained, opening another door to reveal a water closet and washstand. "And this door leads to a porch for sitting a spell. Don't be leaving the door into your room open, though. Mehitabelle likes to sun herself out here, and she'll try to get inside, if she gets a chance."

"Mehitabelle?"

"The house cat."

"I see. I'll be careful. Will she settle for sitting on my lap?"

"If she likes you. That's up to her."

Becca smiled again at his refreshing honesty. The young fellow knew his cats! "I'll try to make friends. Thank you for your help."

"Is there anything else you need, ma'am?"

"Well, you could point me toward the registration center. I'd like to find out if there are any South Carolina troops in attendance."

"It's too late to be going there now. They'll be closing up shop soon. Best save that for the morning. Besides, supper is almost ready. You'll hear the bell when they open the dining room."

With some surprise, Becca realized that she was famished. "Supper sounds like a wonderful idea. Thank you again."

Supper was, indeed, ready. Becca made her way to the dining room, where a motherly woman in an apron handed her a plate. "Evenin', ma'am, and welcome to Gettysburg. Find yourself a place anywhere you see an empty chair. We'll be passing the food just as fast as our ladies in the kitchen can dish it up."

Becca hesitated, her eyes widening as she surveyed the crowded dining room. People jostled for space, and the serving women raised their voices to be heard above the general clamor.

"Mashed potatoes coming through!"

"Who needs another biscuit?"

"More chicken here!"

The woman at the door laughed at her surprised expression. "Yes'm, it's a madhouse. The hotel usually offers a quiet and elegant dining experience, but with this many people in town, all they could do was bring in every available housewife and hope that we could cook fast enough to keep everybody fed. So don't be shy. Get in there and help yourself to whatever anybody passes your way."

Again Becca found herself grinning at the novelty of the experience. Bowls of chicken and dumplings, green beans, fried squash, brown gravy, and sliced tomatoes all tempted her to overfill her plate. Sliced country ham, smothered pork chops, fried chicken, and ears of corn followed. After her long day on the train, everything tasted wonderful. The gentleman next to her poured her a glass of lemonade, and a friendly woman across the table leaned forward to offer some advice.

"We were here last night. Be sure to save room for dessert. They make wonderful pies and chocolate cakes."

"There's nothing like country cooking, is there?" Becca replied. The last remnants of her fears about the trip faded away as she settled into the homey atmosphere.

* * *

In the morning, she had barely found a seat at one of the community tables when Tom arrived, greeting her with a warm hug and the usual questions about her trip.

"It was smooth and uneventful, Thomas, and my room is lovely, too. I could get used to those electric lights. But I wasn't expecting to see you here. Surely you haven't made the journey simply on my account?"

"Well, not completely. Our investment firm holds shares in this hotel, and this is perhaps the biggest week the business will ever experience. Someone needed to keep an eye on how the staff is coping, so I volunteered—killing the proverbial two birds with one stone, you might say."

"I'm grateful. The crowds out there on the street are a little intimidating. A familiar face is most welcome."

"I have the use of a small car, so after breakfast, we'll set out to find whatever you need to see. But first, let me fix you a plate of eggs and sausages. You'll need lots of energy before this day is over."

Fueled by the hearty breakfast, Becca was ready to find some answers to her questions. Tom confirmed her impression that the returning veterans would be signing in to locate the tents designated for their units. "The folks managing the camp are headquartered over at Gettysburg College, so that's where we will start."

Although it was still early, the narrow streets of Gettysburg bustled with foot traffic as well as vehicles and horse-drawn carriages. Among the visitors and sightseers dressed in everyday clothes, bands of grizzled soldiers wearing their old uniforms practiced their marching and greeted one another with hugs and backslaps.

"What a mass of humanity," she commented. "How many people . . .?"

"The responses indicated some 50,000 veterans would be coming, and some officials expect at least that many more civilian visitors. It's a tremendous load to put on this little town of less than 5,000 residents. Almost every house is offering their spare rooms, and churches and schools are prepared to house the overflow as well. That's why I took the liberty of reserving early a room for you in a comfortable hotel."

* * *

At the makeshift headquarters of the encampment, Becca managed to catch the attention of a kindly woman behind a desk littered with handwritten account books.

"Can you tell me how to go about finding the friends of two soldiers who fought here?" she asked.

"Union or Confederate?"

"Confederate."

"Do you know their regiment?"

"7th Regiment, South Carolina Volunteers."

"Name and rank?"

"Oh, dear, the older one was a private, I suppose. His name was Job McKay."

The woman busied herself for some time, flipping pages in one of the registers and then turning to a bank of drawers filled with cards. "No one by that name in our records, ma'am, but we don't know much about the enlisted troops. Most of our records are for the officers. There were some 170,000 men who fought in the battle of Gettysburg, you realize. We have records for less than half of them."

"I understand. I knew it was a long shot. But I was hoping to get some idea of how he died."

"Well, I can tell you that the South Carolina troops were in McLaw's Division, Kershaw's Brigade. Most of them saw action on July 2, around Rose's Farm, the Peach Orchard, and the Wheatfield, so most of the South Carolina veterans are housed—or tented, as the case may be—in that area. But beyond that, I don't . . ."

"Is there a map? I don't know any of these place names."

"I'd recommend that you try to find someone to guide you around the battleground. Most of our volunteer guides are checking in right over there," the woman said, pointing to another desk swarming with people. "Any of them who are available will be hanging around that desk." She gave Becca an apologetic shrug and a smile before turning to the next person in line.

"'Scuse me, ma'am. Sorry to eavesdrop, but maybe I can be of assistance. Sergeant Hiram R. Jones, 7th SCV, at your service, ma'am."

Becca whirled around to find herself face-to-face with a bewhiskered old soldier dressed in the faded and tattered butternut-gray uniform of the Confederate Army. Above the right breast pocket she could faintly make out the stenciled name "H.R. Jones" and the regimental designation "7 SCV."

"You are . . . really . . . a veteran from South Carolina?"

"Yes, ma'am. Joined up in Abbeville in 1861, fought in every battle up till . . . well, till I couldn't fight no more."

"Abbeville! I lived in Aiken during the war. Did you by any chance know my friend Job McKay from there? He was in the 7th Regiment, Company E, I believe."

"McKay? Let me think. McKay. I do remember a fellow from over that way. Carrot top, was he?"

"Yes! He and his brothers all had bright red hair—and freckles, a whole band of them across their noses."

"Yes, ma'am. I remember him now. And he had a funny name, too. Uriah, I think it was. He tried going by his initials, but that just led to more jokes. You know—he'd introduce himself as U. R. McKay, and somebody would say, 'No, I'm not McKay, you are.'"

"Ah! He went by his formal name when he signed up? No wonder that lady couldn't find his records! The family always called him Job. They said he had to have the patience of Job to put up with all the teasing about his name."

"Sure. I remember him now, but . . . didn't he get himself killed here?"

"That's what I was told, but no one talked about the details. I was hoping I could find . . . could learn what happened . . . could come to understand . . ."

"I don't know anyone can really understand what happens in wartime, ma'am, but I can tell you a little about the battle we were in. Care to go for a bit of a walk, do you? Mind, it's probably several miles from here."

Tom had been standing a respectful distance behind her, letting her conduct her own investigation. Now she turned to find him and took his arm to make the introductions. "We have a car," she explained. "If you could ride along with us . . ."

"Sure thing. We can travel west on Fairfield Road till we get to the general area of the Confederate camps. Then we'll take the Millerstown Road over to Rose's Farm, where our boys faced the enemy."

* * *

As they drove, the old sergeant studied Becca carefully. "Were you Job's girl?" he asked.

"Oh, no. I wasn't that old. In 1863, I was only thirteen. But I was new in Aiken, didn't know anyone, and Job's little brother befriended me at church. Joshua was, maybe, fifteen—too young, anyhow, to go off to war. But he was feeling very lonely, with his two older brothers off in the army, so we sort of gravitated together. He became my best friend—my only friend, actually. And then his family got the bad news about their oldest son, and Joshua ran off to find his remaining brother."

"Did he ever write to you?"

"Once." She shrugged. "He said he was catching up to Job's unit. Then the next thing we heard, both McKay boys had died at Gettysburg. His parents left town, and I never knew . . ." Her voice trailed off, and she turned quickly to stare out the window.

"Josh McKay. Of course! Who could forget that spunky kid? He came running up to us on the road somewhere around Hagerstown, and we knew right away who he was related to, what with that red hair and freckles. Colonel Aiken wasn't happy to have a youngster among us, but his brother pleaded to let him stay. They finally reached an agreement. The boy would do what he could to help around our encampments, and Job would see to it that he stayed out of any fighting and didn't get in anyone's way. Worked pretty well, at least for a while."

"So you knew him? You know what happened to him?"

"Ah, yes, ma'am, but I'm not sure you . . ."

Becca straightened her back and glared at the old soldier. "Sergeant, I'm much too old to be shocked by anything you have to tell me. I want to hear the whole story, so let's get on with it."

"Fair enough. Our regiment was marching up to Gettysburg from Hagerstown when we spotted a big black building built of fieldstones. It had a sign out front with a black horse painted on it above the word 'Tavern.' Colonel Aiken pointed to a large open field a short distance down the road and announced that we would be camping there. Everybody cheered. Then he explained that he had been assigned to take possession of the tavern to use as a field hospital if we got into a fight."

Becca raised an eyebrow at him. "Really? A tavern?"

"Why not? Its stone walls were practically bullet-proof, it was roomy and situated at a crossroads for good access, and it was almost sure to have a ready supply of medicinal alcohol. If you turn left here, we'll come to it in a few minutes. This whole overgrown area you see on your left is where we set up our camp. We weren't allowed to patronize the tavern that night, but a small cavalry troop frightened the owner off, took control of the building, and did their best to parcel out kegs of beer for each regiment. Before we go to see the tavern, though, let me take you to view our battlefield.

"We learned that there had been fighting in Gettysburg that day, but we were not supposed to join in until the next afternoon. So we got settled, slept some, and then started getting ready for an attack on July 2nd. The 7th was assigned to McLaw's Division, Kershaw's Brigade, and we were part of a very long line assigned to take control of Seminary Ridge and then move east toward the town. We were in position by two o'clock, standing shoulder to shoulder in a single line that stretched for almost fifteen miles. We didn't actually start to move until about five-thirty, though."

"Why so late?"

"Well, it was very hot that day—triple digits, they said—so it helped to fight after the sun started to set. Besides, it just takes a long time to get a fifteen-mile-long line organized."

"And this Seminary Ridge—where is it?"

"You're right on top of it, actually. It's just a bit of high ground that stretches north-south from near here up to the Lutheran Seminary north of town and to the Devil's Den to the south."

"How did it feel to stand there, knowing you were headed into a major battle?"

"Well, we didn't know it was going to be a major battle. And, first, you also need to understand the meaning of that line. When you are waiting for the fighting to start, the world takes on a different aspect, somehow. You quit seeing fields and distant hills, barns, houses, trees. Your vision shrinks, until all you are aware of is the ground beneath your feet and the men standing on either side of you. You are literally touching them, shoulder to shoulder, hip to hip, and you move as a single body. You know that your life depends on them and that their lives depend on you. You become united by a bond of comradeship—love, really—that makes you brave and unafraid. There's no feeling that quite matches it."

"You haven't said anything about love of country, or believing in your cause, or . . ."

"That's because those things don't matter much in the heat of battle. All you care about is staying alive and keeping your comrades alive. So you do whatever it takes, which includes killing your enemies. You don't have time to think about why you are fighting or about the loved ones you left behind, either. People who have never gone to war don't—can't—understand that."

Becca's expression began to crumble, but she once again straightened her posture and said, "All right. Go on. What happened?"

"Well, we were marching across here, headed down the ridge and straight for a line of Union cannons that had only a small infantry line protecting them. They were waiting over there beyond the road. The hope was that we could keep the artillerymen from firing those cannons by picking them off every time they moved. We were in a wooded area and trying to get beyond it, so we could fire our guns without the bullets bouncing off the trees. Then we ended up in Farmer Rose's peach orchard, which wasn't much better. When we broke free of the orchard, we found ourselves in a real fight, but we were only a few hundred yards away from capturing that artillery line. There's a stone wall right over there that gave us some protection, but beyond it was an open, level clover field, and our color guard fell as soon as we emerged from behind the wall.

"Still, it looked like we were winning for a while. We managed to drive the enemy infantry back for almost half a mile. And then came what General Kershaw later described as the fatal blunder. We were still marching shoulder to shoulder, closing ranks whenever one of our number was hit. Then here came a young officer on horseback, crying out the order, "Wheel right!" So that's what we did." He grimaced at the memory and fell silent for a moment.

"I don't understand what that means. What happens when you . . . wheel right?"

"The line breaks. The first soldier turns to his right ninety degrees. The men next to him—three or four, depending on how wide the field is—move up to stand beside him, and they march on in that new direction. Then the next man turns to form a new row. And so on. Now instead of a single unified line, you have men marching in a wide column. And instead of facing those cannons, we were now facing sideways from them. So we couldn't fire at the artillery men, while they had a clear shot at our whole flank."

"The order was the fatal blunder?"

"Yep. We later learned that it was meant for a small group of men who were marching in the wrong direction. But the young signal corpsman heard it, thought it was a general order, and passed it all down the line. We didn't know. We just did what we were told. The Yankees blew us away, mowed us down like they were taking target practice. When we moved out of the range of one cannon, we marched directly into the next line of fire. In our one regiment, we had eighteen killed outright and many more mortally wounded. Another sixteen lost an arm or a leg. And some were knocked unconscious by the blasts. A hundred or more suffered lesser wounds, which is what happened to me. I had a hole in my left shoulder and a gash in my left leg, but I was still upright, at least for a while. Most weren't.

"We finally made it to the wheat field on the other side, where an earlier battle had driven the Yankees out, but by then it was getting dark. The order came to lie down and spend the night right where we were in order to hold the ground, which meant trying to sleep amidst dead bodies."

"Nobody removed those who had been killed?"

"No point in doing that. Eventually, they would be buried where they had fallen, some of them under those same peach trees. But the immediate need was getting the wounded carried to the rear and to the field hospital for medical attention. If you'll drive us a little further west down the next road, Mr. Maloney, I'll show you the tavern. It's still there."

It was a bigger building than Becca had expected, nearly three stories high, its walls solid and almost unbroken with windows. It loomed over the crossroads, still displaying the "Black Horse" sign to invite travelers to stop. Trees sheltered it in the back and partially concealed the smaller house and farm buildings that surrounded it.

"I see why someone would think the crossroads made a good location for a hospital."

"Yes, true, but by the time we got our men moved all the way back here, it was full to bursting. We had to take our wounded boys across the road and lay them out in the shelter of those trees you see. Just beyond, there's the Marsh Creek, which is actually more of a river than a creek. It's deep and fast flowing, though, so it was a good source of drinking water, and the trees offered some protection from the hot sun. Nevertheless, it was hard on the wounded to lie there, waiting to be moved into the tavern for treatment."

"And Job?"

"Job was one of the most seriously wounded. Poor fellow. He had been promoted to corporal that very day but hadn't had the time or opportunity to sew on his new insignia before he fell. He had a deep wound in his abdomen and had lost a lot of blood. Little Josh was right there when we carried him in, and I found myself yelling at the boy for trying to use his shirt as a bandage for his brother's wound. I told him it would get cold after nightfall, and he would need his own shirt. But Josh said his brother needed it more."

The sergeant stopped talking, a faraway look in his eyes.

"That sounds like something my Josh would do. Please. What happened then?"

"I don't know that you need to hear the rest, ma'am."

"I do. Go on."

"In the morning, Job was still alive and calling for water. Josh took his canteen down to the creek to refill it. On the way back, he got stopped by two renegade Yankees, fellows not in uniform but definitely looking for trouble. They asked the boy if he was a Yank or a Rebel, and Josh pulled his shoulders back, declared himself to be a South Carolina soldier and proud of it. So they . . . they shot him."

"No!" Becca could not control her cry.

"Sorry, ma'am. Job saw the whole exchange and struggled to pull himself upright. Then he fell backward, dead from the effort."

"So the Yankees killed both of them." Her voice was bitter. "And what happened to their bodies?"

"We buried them, ma'am, in a real cemetery. It's right over there." The old soldier pointed back across the road, where, not far from the tavern, a stone wall surrounded a small group of tombstones. "That was a private family graveyard, but we buried our dead there, too. Josh and Job are together, in the upper northeast corner. It's kind of overgrown, but you can walk there if you like."

"Yes, I need to do that."

"You two go ahead, then. She'll need some help across the uneven ground, Mr. Maloney. I'll wait for you here. I've already seen all I need of that cemetery."

Becca stood in the graveyard for several minutes, head bowed, as she tried to absorb all the old soldier had told her. Then she turned, taking a deep breath. "That's it. That's what I came for. We can go back now. Thank you for making it possible, Thomas."

As they made their way back, Becca's glance passed over a headstone she had not noticed before. On it was inscribed "Sgt. Hiram R. Jones, 7th SCV, d. July 6, 1863." She grasped Tom's arm in shock. "Wait! Look at this! That's our sergeant."

"Where is he, by the way? We left him standing by the car, but he's nowhere in sight."

"He's gone! You don't think . . ."

"That he was a Gettysburg ghost? Maybe. Or maybe he was just an impersonator. Whoever he was, he brought you the answers you needed. Ready to go home?"

"Yes, indeed, and with a much deeper understanding of what that war was all about."

This selection was previously published as two chapters of Carolyn Schriber's turn-of-the-century novel, Yankee Daughters (Katzenhaus Books, 2016).

Photo by Pat McGrath Avery

Carolyn Schriber

Carolyn Schriber hated history classes when she was growing up because they required little but memorization. Once she was so bored by the material that instead of answering an essay exam on the Revolutionary War, she filled in the space by writing several verses of "The Star-Spangled Banner." The professor gave her an A, which may have suggested that he was as tired of names and dates as she was. Or maybe he was just impressed that she knew more than the first verse. Eventually, however, she discovered a teacher who was an enthusiastic story-teller, and her love of history blossomed.

Now a retired history professor, Schriber spends her free time doing what she loves best, next to teaching—writing about the stories behind the history. She draws her inspiration from the soft warmth of the South Carolina Low Country and the cool, crisp mountain air of western Pennsylvania. In her books she tries to identify themes that reach across the borders of time and geography to penetrate the human heart. And as might be expected of a long-time cat lover, almost every story has its own cat.

Four of her books have received medals from the Military Writers Society of America and in 2015 she was named their "Author of the Year."

Photo by Pat McGrath Avery

Photo by Pat McGrath Avery

SEVEN

Understandings

Christopher Avery

Recently, I took a trip to Gettysburg National Park. It was my second trip to Gettysburg. I had gone there for the first time about seven years ago. I was amazed by the enormity of the battlefield. Now, here is the thing. I had spent a good part of my life reading about the Civil War and about that battle specifically. I didn't know it all but I was knowledgeable. I could recite all the generals, all the units present, the numbers (casualties), and where they engaged. Needless to say, I was excited to be there. For the first time, looking over that battlefield, I was intimidated by the magnitude and I felt so small and so insignificant. I stood from mountaintop or valley, it didn't matter, and felt that, in 1863, a person must have felt like a speck, too insignificant to matter in the grand scheme. I walked across that stretch of field, over three quarters of a mile, that made up Pickett's Charge. I was amazed by how large the field was, how tiny the line of trees, the targets, were on the other side. I imagined the large, expansive movements that 12,500 men would make to arrive on the other side in tandem with one another.

I was lucky enough this visit to attend some lectures about the battle and the area. These lectures varied from the technology, or medicine, all the way to the fashion of the day. I learned about the daily life of the soldier, the uniform that he (or she) wore, the weapons used, and the food eaten by the two armies. In short, I learned more about the minutia of the day than the overall scope of the battle. In these lectures, I learned about the individuals who fought in the war.

One of the lectures that I most enjoyed was about two friends from the same town who fought in the war. The speaker obviously loved history, that much was evident, in the way that he revealed the story of these two men. He was visibly moved by the fates of people he had never met. There it was. It hit me right then. Throughout my life, I had wondered about the supply lines, the firepower, the general's abilities on either side. Time not wasted, mind you, history is history, and there is grandeur in those broad strokes that paint history.

MWSA Gettysburg Writers' Retreat

On our way to Gettysburg, one of the prime topics of conversation had been on Robert E. Lee, the famous leader of the Confederate armies. We discussed his character, his loyalty, and his motivation. Some thought him a traitor and some did not. Lee resigned his commission in the US Army to fight against it. A traitor, right? Pure and simple. He had sworn to fight against all enemies, foreign and domestic and he was taking up arms against his own nation. A revered leader to some, and perhaps the greatest symbol of the romantic lost cause of the Confederacy. A man who had fought in the Mexican War of 1848, who had moved against John Brown at Harper's Ferry, but could not, in good conscience, raise his arms against his beloved Virginia. One could argue that due to the technology of the times, man had more of a connection to a state or local governments than to the federal. Were General Lee and the men of the Confederacy traitors or patriots? Fighting for slavery, fighting for state's rights, were they just? That is a question that doesn't come easily, if at all. However, those were the thoughts as I arrived in Gettysburg. Questions that had become more relevant to me personally as I learned that my direct ancestors served in the 24th Virginia, which participated in Pickett's Charge.

I have at least four, and maybe five ancestors who served in the 24th Virginia. The fifth, and a possible sixth is unverified at the time of this writing. Four, for sure, enlisted in the 24th Virginia and three, for sure, participated in the battle as one died previous to the battle. The 24th Virginia formed the extreme right of Pickett's Charge. They reached the stone wall which is considered to be the "high water mark" of the Confederacy. The 24th Virginia was one of only two units that participated in the charge that did not lose their regimental colors. They suffered a 40% casualty rate during the battle. In fact, of the 1300 men who served with the regiment during the war, only 9 were left to surrender at Appomattox.

On the last day of the visit, I walked across that field again. This time knowing that my ancestors had tread on that same ground. It couldn't have been more different. Sure, the field was still huge and the group of trees seemed so small and far away. It was still three quarters of a mile of open ground to cover, but this time walking the same ground as my ancestors — I felt different. Everything was closer, the sun seemed closer, shining down, the hills to the front and to the right seemed closer, raining down cannon fire on the men of the 24th. Everything seemed closer, in fact, except that mathematically, they still had a 3/4 mile to cover. I knew that General Longstreet had been right. No 15,000 men ever made could have taken that ridge. I reached those trees knowing that I had walked the same distance that I had walked seven years ago but felt differently.

In researching the family tree, I find that we had members on both sides. I imagine that is common. It is, after all, a civil war. I don't have any more answers the second time that I took that walk—only more questions. I am convinced that neither side was completely right. One upheld the institution of slavery and the other was an invading country. I don't know which side that I would have been on. I really don't. I am from Kansas City, Missouri. The Governor of the state was pro-union, while most of my neighbors in the western part of the state would have been southern sympathizers who were being raided by the abolitionists in neighboring Kansas. 150 years later, feelings still run deep. It goes back to General Lee. The government you swore to protect or the state you love. I can't imagine, ever fighting for slavery but I can't ever imagine raising my hand against my friends and neighbors either.

Photo by Pat McGrath Avery

Photo by Pat McGrath Avery

Christopher Avery

Chris has loved history his entire life. The Civil War has always held a special interest for him.

He graduated from Rockhurst University and has continued to enjoy literature and history.

Photo by Pat McGrath Avery

Photo by Joyce Faulkner

Maggie Abbott, Historian and Speaker

Historian, Author, and Speaker, Dale Fetzer

Photo by Joyce Faulkner

EIGHT

A Cousin's Promise

Dwight Jon Zimmerman

XII Corps Field Hospital
A Farm Somewhere Near Culp's Hill
July 3, 1863, Early Afternoon

"All right, Sam, take him away and bring me another," U.S. Army Surgeon Latimer Wilson said as he finished stitching up the right stump of a leg amputated just above the knee. Wilson then stepped back as Corporal Samuel Harris and Private Walter Pennyworth set their litter beside the chloroformed body of a major from Brigadier General Thomas Kane's Second Brigade, Second Division, lifted him onto it, and carried him off the wooden barn door that served as Dr. Wilson's operating table.

An orderly pressed into the doctor's hands a cup of coffee as litter bearers brought up his next patient, a wounded sergeant. His marathon of surgery began at what seemed a lifetime ago, sometime after sunset on July 1. He and his hospital wagon train were on the Baltimore Pike heading north to Gettysburg when he heard gunfire coming from Culp's Hill.

Immediately he ordered the wagon train to stop and set up station at a farm bordering the Baltimore Pike. Dr. Wilson then woke up the surprised owner and informed him that a medical team of the XII Corps of the Army of the Potomac had just requisitioned his farm for a field hospital.

Dr. Wilson had taken his action none too soon. Before the last tent had been raised, the first in a long line of wounded soldiers appeared. The initial trickle quickly became an onrush so great that Wilson ordered the barn doors taken down and turned into makeshift operating tables as well. There in the farmyard under a sky where ominous storm clouds were gathering, Dr. Latimer Wilson and his men went to work.

The rush of caffeine from the coffee only partially alleviated Dr. Wilson's exhaustion. As orderlies prepared his next patient, a sergeant, for surgery, Dr. Wilson looked around at the bloody detritus that is the terrible aftermath of battle.

Closest to the Baltimore Pike was the farm's wooden barn. Attached to its west side was a rail fence, or what was left of it after his men and the wounded had arrived. Beside the stone farm house were a wooden outhouse and two out buildings, a granary and storage shed, also of stone. A couple of large oaks dominated the site.

Instead of setting up in the barn, Dr. Wilson decided to do the operating in the open air under a canvas canopy. Close to the operating tables and lying under additional canopies were the wounded awaiting medical attention, which is to say in the overwhelming majority of cases meant amputation of one sort or another. Scattered about wherever there was free space under some shelter, whether in the barn or outbuildings, under their eaves or trees lay those who had been treated and were lying in recovery.

Where previously the farm echoed with the lowing of cows, grunts of pigs, clucks and crows of chickens and rooster, and barking of dogs, now the air was filled with moans, whimpers, and shrieks of men in agony. The only place quiet was behind the barn, near the turnoff onto the Baltimore Pike. There lay a group forever at peace: the dead.

Dr. Wilson handed the empty cup to an orderly and wiped his bloody hands on his equally bloody apron. As he stepped toward his makeshift operating table, the tip of his boot touched something. Looking down, he saw it was the lower right leg that moments earlier had belonged to the major.

"Sam, have someone gather up this and the other reminders of my 'surgical skill' for burial before I find myself knee deep in them."

"I'll do it, doctor," the corporal replied, bending down to pick up hands, arms, and legs and drop them in a nearby wheelbarrow set aside for the purpose. When it was full he lifted it by the handles and headed toward the back of the barn where beside the dead he would complete his gruesome mission.

Dr. Wilson, meanwhile, turned to address his latest patient. He looked down and stared in sad recognition at the arm with an all-too-familiar wound. The minié ball had struck where the ulna and radius joined the wrist, shattering them. The good news, such as it were, was that the sergeant stood a better than average chance of surviving the amputation.

"Prepare to administer the chloroform, Jim," he said.

Sergeant James Kraft looked up from the medicine cabinet and said, "Doctor, we're out of chloroform. So many wounded came in so fast—no one had time to get more."

"Damn," Dr. Wilson muttered. He leaned over to talk to the sergeant. "What's your name, sergeant?"

"Johnson, doctor," he gasped through gritted teeth. "Thomas Johnson."

"Sergeant Johnson, I'm afraid I'm going to have to amputate your hand without the help of chloroform. I promise you I'll work fast. It should take less than ten minutes. But, I won't lie to you. Without the chloroform to make you unconscious, what I'm going to do will hurt like the devil. I'll have to have four men hold you down while I operate."

Sergeant Johnson's sweat-soaked face was steaked with gunpowder and blood. Wincing in pain, he whispered, "It already hurts like hell, doctor. I've gotten this far. I think I can survive a little more."

Dr. Wilson nodded to four orderlies picked for this duty because of their size and brawn. They took their positions around the sergeant's body and grabbed a limb in an iron grip. A moment later the early afternoon air, already filled with the sound of suffering, was rent with a deafening bellow of a man in acute pain.

* * *

"Corporal, I've been told that Major Benjamin Chandler was taken here. Where might I find him?"

Though the back wall of the barn separated Corporal Harris and the dead from the wounded on the other side, he and they were in full view of anyone coming off the Baltimore Pike. He looked up from the hole he was digging and saw sitting on a one-horse buggy a dark-haired, attractive, well-dressed woman of medium build who appeared to be in her mid-thirties. What caught and held his attention was the intense, almost hypnotic gaze of her deep blue eyes.

"Ma'am," he said, waving his hand at the sight around him, and nodding toward the farmyard. "You shouldn't be here. It's not a place for a lady such as yourself."

"Young man," she said in a level voice that held an undercurrent of command, "I am a midwife and mistress of a farm. Between delivering babies and butchering livestock I have witnessed my share of blood."

Nodding at the nearby dead bodies and the wheelbarrow of severed limbs, she said, "As for tragedy, I've guided more than one mother-to-be through the agony of labor only to reap the reward of a babe stillborn—and then to tell their menfolk that not only are they not fathers, neither are they any longer husbands, instead widowers.

"I'll stay."

Embarrassed, Corporal Harris nodded and dropped his gaze. "Yes, ma'am," he said.

Suddenly one of the farmer's wandering dogs lunged up onto the wheelbarrow, snatched in his jaws a forearm, and raced away.

"I think it prudent you dig a deep hole," she said wryly. "I see this farmer also has pigs."

"Yes, ma'am," he said. "Uh, the major you asked about? I don't know if he's the one you want, but Dr. Wilson a little while ago amputated the leg off a major. He was taken to the granary over there." And he pointed to a group of men lying under the eaves of the stone granary.

"Thank you, corporal," she said, snapping her reins, and guiding her horse to where he indicated. Upon reaching it she stopped and stepped off the buggy, looped the reins over the horse's head, tied them to the horse anchor provided by the blacksmith from where she had rented her rig and dropped the iron anchor onto the ground. She briefly primped herself before walking toward the soldiers.

They lay on the ground in an even row, some missing hands and arms, some missing feet and legs, and a few otherwise whole with bodies swathed in bandages where bullets, shrapnel, or both had torn into their flesh. Conversations and moans of pain stopped when they saw her. The soldiers looked at her in varying states of puzzlement and interest. Her attire told them she was from a social status different from the women they normally encountered. As she walked down the line, she paused before each man and looked him straight in the face. Though she said not a word, her eyes silently conveyed her compassion for his condition before moving on. Then, she found him.

Like an island of tranquility in the middle of a mortal sea of pain and turmoil, Major Benjamin Chandler lay quietly on the ground, his chest slowly rising and falling, seemingly asleep.

She gathered her skirts and knelt beside him. She looked at the stump with its hastily-stitched skin flap covering the raw wound. Her nostrils flared briefly as she caught the hint of an all-too-familiar scent.

A pair of privates arrived carrying an amputee on a litter and lay him beside the others. "Ma'am," one of them said. "Do you have authorization to be here? If you're not from the Sanitary Commission, you'll have to leave."

She looked at the private and fixed him with a gaze that sent a cold chill down his spine. "I am here to keep a promise to my cousin, Major Benjamin Chandler's wife," she said. "Leave me be." The private gulped in fear and quickly stumbled away.

Elizabeth Anne "Bess" Dillard then gently took the comatose major's hands in hers, took a deep breath, closed her eyes . . .

. . . and walked through an opaque barrier and onto a fog-shrouded, featureless plain.

Somewhere behind the mists on her left she heard the sound of someone pounding against something and shouting, "Damn you! Open up! Let me back, I say! Open!"

She walked toward the sound. The mists parted to reveal Major Chandler, whole of body, his fists impotently assailing the barrier.

"You're not going to get through it, Ben," she said.

At the sound of her voice, Major Chandler stopped. "I should, Bess, there's so much yet left to do."

Taking a deep breath, he turned to face her. "When did you know?" he asked. Then, quickly raising his hand, he said, "Don't answer. It's one of your gifts; one of the reasons why some call you the Witch of Warwoman Creek."

"That is one of my names," she replied, smiling. "Said behind my back."

Waving his hand at the mist, he said, "This is familiar territory for you, isn't it, Bess?" Then, looking down at his right leg he asked, "How much did he cut off?"

"Just above the knee."

Major Chandler stared at his right leg pensively. "Well, he tried." Then he returned his attention to her. "You're here to carry out that promise you made to Winnie when I rode off to war," he said.

"You may call me the Angel of Death. It is your right."

He stared hard at her in silence. "Whatever you are, witch . . . angel . . . of death?" He looked at his hands. "No. These are the hands employed in the business of dealing out death. Not yours."

With that statement a decade of years was shed from the form of the fifty-two-year-old man.

"When will it happen?"

"That is for you to choose."

"Do I make any final confession to you?"

"Also, for you to choose."

"What happens after this?"

"Again, something for you to choose."

"Winnie . . ." he whispered. Upon uttering the name of his wife, another decade vanished from his form.

"Did I ever tell you that you are beautiful? All those years I've known you, you've never aged."

"It's kind of you to say that."

"Has anyone ever fought you . . . over here?"

"When I journey to this place? Sometimes they resist at first. But, no, no one has ever fought me."

"That's because the fighting all happens over there," he said, pointing at the barrier. "On the other side." When he

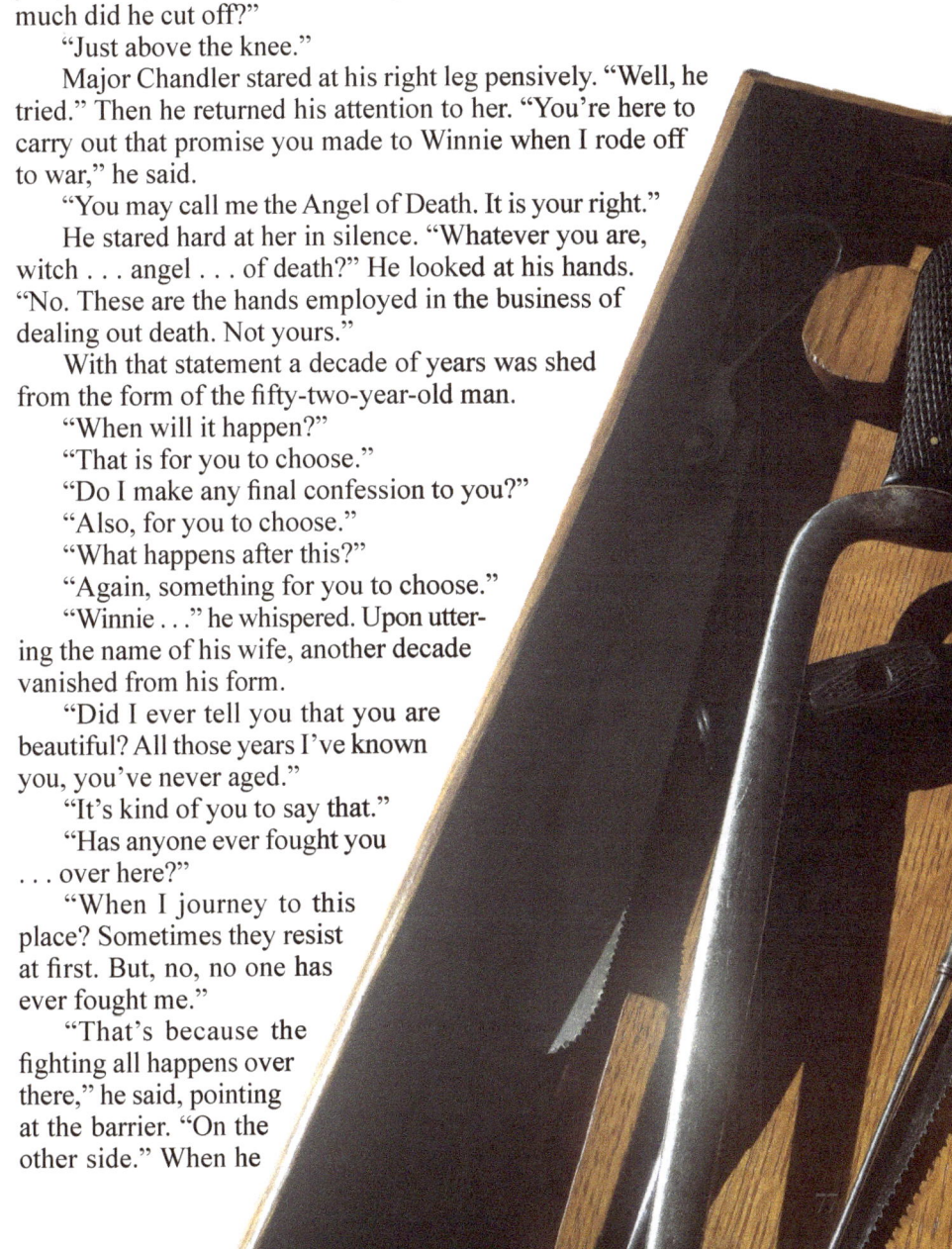

returned to look at her again, it was through the eyes of a twenty-two-year-old. He looked down at his youthful body.

"Is this your doing?"

"No, it's yours."

"I won't remember any of this, will I?"

She shook her head slightly in the negative.

Ben, now twelve years old, looked up at her with gleaming eyes. "I'm so happy to meet you! You are an angel! You are!"

She smiled, tears welling in her eyes. A soft glow began to appear around him. The now six-year-old boy looked at the glow as it surrounded him. Turning to her he said solemnly, "It's almost time, isn't it?"

She nodded, unable to speak.

"What's your name?" The glow was now brighter.

"Elizabeth—Bess."

"What do I say, Angel Bess?" The glow's intensity increased.

Elizabeth Anne Dillard got on her knees before the four-year-old and took his hands in hers. "You say, farewell."

As the now blinding glow began to engulf him, he said, "Farewell, Angel Bess."

"Farewell, Ben." She tenderly kissed him once on each cheek . . .

. . . and folded the hands of Major Benjamin Chandler onto his unmoving chest.

Photo by Joyce Faulkner

Dwight Jon Zimmerman

DWIGHT JON ZIMMERMAN is a #1 New York Times bestselling author, editor and president of the Military Writers Society of America. He has written more than a dozen books, including Lincoln's Last Days, the #1 New York Times bestselling adaptation of Killing Lincoln by Bill O'Reilly, and Uncommon Valor: The Medal of Honor and the Warriors Who Earned It in Afghanistan and Iraq which won the 2010 Military Writers Society of America Founder's Award, the organization's highest honor. He has written more than 300 articles on military history, as well as comic book stories for Marvel Comics and other comic book publishers. Zimmerman has lectured at the U.S. Military Academy at West Point and the Naval War College, and has appeared on the FOX programs DEFCON-3 hosted by K.T. McFarland, and AMERICA NEWS HQ discussing military subjects. He lives in Brooklyn, New York, with his wife Joëlle. They have two adult children.

Photo Pat McGrath Avery

Sachs Bridge Photo by Pat McGrath Avery

NINE

Retreat

Pat McGrath Avery

My body is weighted down in defeat,
my heart heavy with sorrow, my soul weary,
weary of war without end, of watching brothers die
while the world goes on. Barely remembering
the passion of my long-erased youth, the fervor
of protecting my southern roots.

I killed Yankees, consumed with the hate
of the battlefield, only to know they were men
like me, filled with dreams of loved ones
at home, fighting for the life they know. Why do
we turn to battle to settle our differences?
Why can we not let others live in peace?

Why must my comrades and I march to fight again?
What about our brothers left behind? Will they
ever find rest beneath their southern soil? Why do I
put one foot in front of the other to reach this bridge?
Would not it be better to drown in the creek below
than to face another battle?

But a flicker of hope seeks entry into my tortured soul
and aching body as I hear the clatter of my comrades'
boots and see them moving forward, alive but
unknowing of what lies ahead. I too struggle, but I raise my head
as I slowly shuffle into the
fleeting cocoon of the Sachs Bridge

Pat McGrath Avery

Pat is an author and photographer. In both, she strives to bring a flicker of light and a moment of joy into people's lives.

Photo by Pat McGrath Avery

Photo by Pat McGrath Avery

TEN

Two Points of View

Bob Doerr

The old veteran sat in the restaurant while the proprietor and a young girl cleaned up around him. All the other customers had gone, and Scott knew the girl had already hung the closed sign on the door. A few pedestrians strolled by the restaurant not caring to look in through the window. The girl smiled at him as she swept the floor under a nearby table. A bit scrawny, he thought, but he'd bet she'd turn into a pretty woman. Most of these Pennsylvania girls did. He guessed that the man was her father and from his accent that his ancestors came from Germany.

The kitchen odors had all but dissipated. He drank the last of his coffee and stood up. His left leg ached, but the pain had been with him so long now that he accepted it as normal. In the war when it happened, he thought he might lose the leg. He tossed a tip onto the table, bringing a bigger smile from the girl.

"Come again," the proprietor said without making eye contact.

The veteran almost asked him what he thought about the recent election but caught himself from speaking. Politics, he knew, was never a good topic to discuss with strangers, and a lot of animosity still surrounded the one that just happened. Besides, truth be told, the veteran hadn't liked either of the nation's choices.

He stepped out of the restaurant into the cool night air and shivered. He wondered if he did so because of the night air or the realization that he had returned here for the first time in forty some years. He had stayed away on purpose and now felt like he had returned to the scene of the crime. Perhaps he had.

The city didn't look anything like he remembered. Of course, he knew there was no reason why it should. A lot of time had passed and he didn't catch the city at a good time. Scott walked to his hotel studying the faces of those he passed or saw in a window. He scoffed at his anxiety, but memories have a way of their own to resist being forgotten, and his life had changed in many ways since the last time his feet walked here.

At the hotel he sat in his room and wondered if he shouldn't leave at first light. Although he knew the chances were close to zero, he didn't want to be recognized. He didn't want to explain why he had done what he had. He didn't want to speak of the one action in his life that had tormented him more than any other. Not one action, he said to himself, but a series of events that happened over a handful of days and that still haunted him decades later.

Despite the urge to leave, Scott ate breakfast at the hotel and steeled himself for the task ahead. The walk to the cemetery didn't affect him like the walk to the hotel the night before. He did not find himself scrutinizing the faces he passed. Rather visions, hallucinations, perhaps they were memories flooded his mind. He entered the cemetery grounds, at first not even realizing he had reached his goal. He sat on a bench and tried to gather his thoughts.

Tears came to his eyes, but Scott felt more guilt than sorrow. He wanted to flee and thought he might until he saw her. She seemed to appear from a gravesite. She stood up and walked to another grave and knelt down disappearing behind another headstone. She stood back up and Scott saw that she had flowers in her left hand. She must be placing flowers on the graves, but her face, not what she was doing, grabbed Scott's attention. It couldn't be.

The woman continued leaving a flower at each gravesite and slowly worked her way closer to Scott. More memories flooded his mind, and his emotions once again boiled through his blood. The woman he remembered was a lot younger. This couldn't be her. Then he laughed to himself, and for the first time since coming back, he smiled. He, too, had aged a lot since then. He stared at the woman wanting her to look up and recognize him. He knew that she might not. He had been just one more soldier, but she had saved his life and sent him on a journey that had worked out very well. He had become wealthy and respected, but the shadow of guilt for leaving had never left him. He had made this trip to help cleanse his soul of that guilt.

The woman stood up barely ten paces away from him. She wiped her brow and pulled her shoulder length grey hair back behind her where she did something to fasten it away from her face. Her eyes met his and froze.

"Amber," he said softly. "Is that really you?"

She didn't speak at first. Could this be him? The young soldier she had fallen so hard for so many years ago? The same one who still snuck into her dreams. She saw that his eyes smiled as much as his lips, and she suddenly knew.

"Nick? Nicolas Scott, could that be you?" she asked, her voice barely reaching him.

"Yes. My God, I can't believe it's really you." He stood up and took a few unsteady steps toward her.

She rushed toward him and they embraced. She looked at his face and touched the old scar that ran from his eyebrow into his hairline. "It healed just fine. You're still a handsome man."

Scott laughed. "Please, let's sit down. I have a million questions for you."

They both sat on the bench and Amber put her hand on Scott's wrist like he was a friend she saw every day.

"It's nice of you to bring flowers out here. Do you do it often?" he asked, skirting around all the things he wanted to ask and say.

"Only a few times a year. You know I helped bury some of the boys."

"I remember. I remember thinking that I would be one of them."

"I remember thinking that, too. Those were horrible days. You were my blessing. You helped me survive," she said.

"I think it was the other way around," Scott said, confused at her comment. "I should have lost my leg, if not my life. So many of my brothers did."

"Seeing you alive and well is like a dream come true. I still can't believe you're here." She squeezed his wrist a little tighter. "Despite how much you recovered that week, I worried you might have died from your injuries after you left. I saw so much death that week. You were my one hope."

"We both saw too much death. I only fought in that first day, and yet I saw thousands of my brothers cut down."

"It was the bloodiest conflict of the war. Too many on both sides died," she said.

"No more war talk. How have you been since then? I thought you would have moved away."

"I did. I got married a few years after the war and moved with my husband to Pottstown. We had two sons. They both live in Philadelphia and are doing well. My husband passed away three years ago, and I moved back here. It was just like I needed to come home. How about you? Did you ever marry?"

He noticed that she had glanced at his hand.

"Long ago I married a woman from New York. I lived in Chicago at the time. In fact, I lived there for nearly twenty years after the war. Didn't end up there right away. In fact after leaving here, I spent almost a year in a small Quaker settlement. I had a relapse a few days after I left here. They took me in. They also wanted to amputate my leg. Fortunately, I was conscious enough to argue against that," he smiled at his own remark. "Funny how I can look back and smile about things like that."

"Your wife?"

"She developed pneumonia and passed away in a matter of days. I wasn't ready for that."

"How could you be?" Amber asked. "No one prepares for the unexpected."

Scott remained quiet for a moment. "It's been nearly a year now, and in the last month, I started thinking about coming back here."

"Well, I'm glad you did," she said not knowing if she should say something about his wife's death or not. "Had you not thought about coming back before?"

"Yes, but I've always been afraid of coming back."

"Afraid? Because of the injuries and all the death?"

"No," Scott said, "because of the shame."

Amber scooted away from him and looked at him like she was trying to see some explanation on his face. "The shame? What are you talking about?"

"Thousands of my brothers in the 1st Division died in those three days. Thousands more died later in the war. I deserted them. I ran and fled because I was afraid."

"No you didn't," she said. "You couldn't have fought anymore. You couldn't walk. You could barely see out of your left eye. They left you to die."

"They left me because the southern boys drove them out of the city."

"Two days later, the confederate soldiers returned south. The army knew where they left you, but no one came back to see what happened to you."

"Only the doc would've known where I was, and he may have been killed or wounded or simply swamped with so much death and dying that he forgot about me," he said.

"Maybe. There was a lot of death here. If they came back they would have taken that leg, and your chance of surviving that was slim. We both knew that."

"Yes. That terrified me as much as dying. You gave me better treatment than I would've gotten from them," he said and placed his hand over hers.

"I only did what I watched them do a hundred, maybe a thousand times that week. I just didn't amputate. You know the pile of limbs outside the window in the house they used reached the level of the window before someone took them away to bury or burn them."

Scott shook his head at the thought. "Why did I run away?"

"You didn't run, although I wished you would've stayed. You rode away on a rather small mule. You looked a bit ridiculous, but it was the only thing you could get on," she smiled at the memory. "I worried that you had left too early."

"I had. Like I mentioned, after a few days I relapsed. But why didn't I simply report back to my unit? That has bothered me to this day. I have tried to be the best man that I could be since then to atone for my cowardice," he buried his face in his hands.

"Shame on you, Private Scott," she said and reached her hand out lifting his chin until his eyes met hers. "You were never a coward. The war had moved on. It didn't last another year. You could no longer fight. You served and you fought. You nearly died. You should have a medal, not guilt."

"It's not that simple," he said.

"No, it's not. I urged you not to go back to your unit. You thought you had no choice but to return to the army, even after they had left. I pleaded with you not to."

"I remember that, but that's no excuse."

"But it is. You need to understand. You were the only person I saved in all that hell. I didn't think they would ever send you back into battle, but the thought of that possibility terrified me. That's why I pushed so hard for you to stay or to go north away from the fighting."

"You did save me. You were my guardian angel and are still the only thing that makes me smile about this place."

"Your guilt is irrational. We were both scared. Terrified. What you went through and I witnessed was slaughter on a grand scale. Your commander would have discharged you on the spot if he had seen you, but they left. Only a small contingent stayed behind."

"But why didn't I go to them? Why didn't I return to duty? It was an act of cowardice and betrayal."

She could see the tears fight to get out of his eyes. "Stop blaming yourself. I urged you to go north away from the fighting. Your mind wasn't exactly in perfect working condition. If you need to blame someone, blame me. And don't forget I filled you with whatever medicine I could scrounge. That had to affect your mind. You said yourself you relapsed a few days later. By the time you were back to your right state of mind, the war was probably over."

"It's not that simple," he said again.

"Yes it is. You served, you fought, and you suffered very serious battle wounds," she said and realized the conversation had gone in a big circle. "I've met a lot of veterans that have guilt over not dying. I can understand the feelings exist even if I can't appreciate why anyone would feel that way."

"I know it's irrational, too, but I still feel it," he said.

She smiled at him. "Can I still remember your leaving as the one good thing I helped accomplish? The one young soldier I helped save and not the one young soldier I encouraged to leave the war and thereby ruining the rest of his life?"

"Don't think that. You did help me survive. The doc retreated from the house with those who could run with him. They did leave me."

She smiled, and he returned the smile.

"I have had a good life. I have a lot to be thankful for. You made that happen, Amber."

"I'm not sure I made anything happen. I just tried my best to keep a young man, my age, stay alive and then escape the horror around us."

He hugged her, and she returned the hug.

"I remember you being there next to me asleep on the floor when I awoke at night," he said.

"My parents helped out, too. It wasn't just me."

MWSA Gettysburg Writers' Retreat

"I remember your mom bringing in soup, but that's about all."

"They were frightened," she said. Not much of an explanation but Scott understood.

"I was going to leave Gettysburg today. Do you mind if I stay for another day or two?" he asked.

"Please do." This time she initiated the hug. She wanted to take care of her soldier a little longer. Maybe she could heal him.

Photo by Pat McGrath Avery

Photo by Pat McGrath Avery

Bob Doerr

Before becoming a full time author, multi-award winning author Bob Doerr specialized in military counterintelligence and criminal investigations for 28 years. His published works include eight mystery/thrillers that have garnered a variety of awards and three fantasy novellas for middle grade readers. One of his Jim West mysteries, No One Else to Kill, was a winner in the 2013 Eric Hoffer Awards. The Military Writers Society of America selected Bob as its Author of the Year for 2013. In short fiction, Bob came in second in the Writers Police Academy Golden Donut Award in 2012.

Photo by Pat McGrath Avery

Photo by Pat McGrath Avery

ELEVEN

This Ghost Stuff

Luke the Detective Dog

When we stayed at the Battlefield B&B in Gettysburg, I frequently heard the words "ghosts" and "haunted." I don't understand most of the chatter that humans seem to love, but I know the important words and phrases, like treat, home, good boy, bedtime and let's go for a ride. When humans talked about ghosts, they usually laughed or made some weird shivery action, so I knew it was a word I should remember. But I'm a dog and I would have forgotten all about it except for one night when we slept in the barn. I have an internal clock so I tell my family when it is bedtime.

First let me tell you that the room was nice, but the bed was even nicer—big, cozy and super comfortable. I like to sleep right in the middle of the bed with my humans on both sides. So we cuddled up for a good night's rest.

In the middle of the night, a door slammed and strange vibes raised the fur on my back. I heard footsteps right above me, but it wasn't that noise that made me take notice. I usually bark to let my family know I am protecting them and I keep barking until they check it out. This time, I barked just once when I heard the door open, but then I grew quiet.

Something was different about these steps. All of a sudden they stopped. The fur on my back still stood on end. I couldn't tell you why, but there was a strangeness in the air. I smelled it and I felt it. I listened for a long time. The footsteps never started again, and no one went back out the door.

It took me a long time to get back to sleep. The next day, my family talked about a ghost and everybody laughed. I just shivered. The lady that owns the place said no one goes in or out of the barn at night. If you were to ask me if the Battlefield B&B is haunted, I couldn't tell you. However, if you visit there, and in the middle of the night your hair stands on end, you've been forewarned.

Photo by Pat McGrath Avery

Luke the Detective Dog

Luke is a friendly six-year-old Bichon who loves to help write books. Even more, he loves events where he gets to meet lots of new people.

Big Fluffy Bed in the Barn at the Battlefield B&B

Photo by Pat McGrath Avery

The 50th anniversary of the battle of Gettysburg, Union (left) and Confederate (right) veterans shake hands at a reunion, in Gettysburg, Pennsylvania.

IMAGE: PUBLIC DOMAIN

TWELVE

An Uncivil War

Jack Woodville London

The war had left them with a certain griping in the guts, a simultaneous cramping and loosening that almost all of them had felt from the first time they had heard a cannon fired. The heat was stifling and their old and faded uniforms were not uniform at all.

They tried to form up behind whoever was left of their leaders, shuffling around on the field, kicking up dust and trampling the wheat under their feet. All of them were ready to cross the fields straight to a copse of trees that could be seen in the far distance. The grays took deep breaths and waited for the order to charge across to their old enemy.

Almost a mile away, across the Emmitsburg Road, the blues experienced the same heat, the same griping of the guts, the same miserable clothing, the dust, the straw in the air, and the anxiety, but none of the effort. All they had to do was wait. It would be a good twenty minutes from the last cannon fire before the grays reached them. All of them knew what to expect. All of them knew what to do. All of them knew that for some of them it might be impossible, and each wondered privately if he would be the one to fail. They stiffened.

Several hundred yards behind the blues, high up along the slope of the ridge, field hospitals had been set up among the thousands of milling soldiers and tents and wagons. The army surgeons had watched the grays assemble across the Emmitsburg Road and knew that the charge was imminent. They ordered their lieutenant to stand out in front of the tents and use field glasses to watch the attack unfold.

At two o'clock a volley of cannon fire boomed from the gray's line. A cannon answered from the blues. A bugle blared out To Arms. Every man prepared for the charge and, on cue, their officers yelled out "Attack!" The last faded flowers of state's rights moved out on foot. Those who could see watched as their old enemies crowded along a stone wall, waiting for them, their flags rippling in the slight breeze, suffering in the same direct sunlight with almost no shade from the pitifully few trees that still lived on the battlefield.

"YI YI YI WAOOO YI" the grays shouted, and a chill went up at the stone wall. The blues had heard it before, and knew what the rebel battle cry meant. Many of them wondered if being there was such a good idea. "WAHOO!"

"What do you see, Lieutenant?" one of the surgeons called out from inside the field hospital. The orderlies and nurses rolled up the tent walls for ventilation but it was still brutally hot. The patients on the tables, victims of sunburn and poison ivy and edema of the legs had fevers, suffered as much from the heat as from their maladies. The medics had covered the vacant tables with army blankets because they were too hot for a wounded or sick man to lay down on, and their medical equipment was kept inside chests with wire screen doors. "What do you see?"

"They're about a hundred yards away, Captain. I think they're going to make it." The lieutenant adjusted his binoculars. "It's not clear what's going on. There's a bunch of flags in the way and the rebs are kicking up so much dust I'm amazed they can see where they're going."

All of them came out to watch, the nurses, the orderlies, the surgeons themselves. It took the grays another ten minutes to cross the last hundred yards. There was a slough near the Emmitsburg Road and the men struggled trying to cross it. Once past the slough there was a slope up to the stone wall that hadn't been obvious until the charging men were on it. The medical staff watched them stagger and trip, some of the men falling to the ground and struggling to get back up to continue the charge. To the men and women in front of the hospital tents the sight was frightening and, at the same time, inspiring in an odd sort of way.

"They're at the wall!" Someone yelled. "They made it!"

The stars and stripes waved back and forth over The Angle. The stars and bars waved back. There was a final volley from a cannon that had been perched far to one side, near where the 121st Pennsylvania had fought. Then the grays reached their hands up to the waiting blues at the rock wall, the waiting blues reached their hands down to help their ancient enemies climb up to join them, and the enormous crowd that had gathered to watch the re-enactment of Pickett's Charge let out a collective roar. It was the high water mark of the Gettysburg Reunion.

Up and down the length of the rock wall, above it and below, beneath the trees and spilling over onto the Emmitsburg Road, onto the paved paths that led from one monument to the next, surrounding the sculpted General Meade astride his sculpted Baldy back on Hancock Avenue, ancient veterans shook hands. The men who had tried to kill each other fifty years before, and survived, bore more the marks of aging than of long-past combat. Their eyes glazed over as they raised hickory walking sticks and pointed out to each other where they had been on the battlefield. They choked up, asking "Where were you?" and answering "I was right over there. Or there."

They wore the blue and grey uniforms they had worn in 1863, and the thinning beards and drooping mustaches that they had begun to grow when they left their homes in 1862, the faded hats that had covered them in rain and cold and freezing snow, and their memories of the friends they had left at The Angle, or on Round Top or in the Wheatfield. Looking back to Seminary Ridge, the men in blue pointed west, a mile away, to the statue of General Lee astride Traveler, gazing over the fields where fifty years ago his divisions had disintegrated and he had lost the war. The men in gray looked with them, and told their enemies the names of the men that had fallen there, the Jebs and Nathans and Seths of Virginia, the Amoses and Zebulons of North Carolina. They looked up. Cameras had been placed on tripods, to photograph them.

"Shake hands," the photographer said. He clicked a shutter and withdrew a silver gelatin plate. "Again, and smile." He clicked another shutter and asked them to face a bit more toward the sun. "How about if you take off your hats? That's it. Hold them up in one hand and wave." Like I'm glad to be here, with my enemy, more than one thought. The photographer thanked them and moved twenty feet further along the stone wall and set up his camera again. The wary smiles between old enemies, the poses, the handshakes were copied up and down the line.

"We lost men too, Reb," one of the ancient blues said. He named his cousin, Joshua, who had been killed at the High Water Mark, and his platoon leader, Alonzo, who lost a leg when the 26th North Carolina reached the wall. "The lieutenant, he died up there on that hill," the blue said, pointing, "where they laid him out in one of them tents for the sawbones to clean up."

The gray who had made it across the field and had shaken his hand jerked it back. He made a noise that may have been a sneeze but probably was a snort. The blue flashed his eyes. The gray glared. They squared off and faced each other and began to raise their knobby fists to their sides. A drum pounded out heavy beats. An army band struck up The Stars and Stripes Forever. Then the blue and the gray couldn't hear each other, so gritted their remaining teeth.

Almost a hundred yards away a Pennsylvania congressman mounted a stage that no one had noticed before. That he had not fought there, nor had his father or brother, was no impediment to his exordium that "the clash fifty years earlier that had taken place at the bloody angle proved to be essential to the American nation."

"And I say to you, valiant veterans of the Great Civil War, that this jubilee on this famous field is the supreme justification of war and of battle. You join in embraces of those who you fought and share your tears above your dead on this very ground where they died, the proof that they did not die in vain…"

He spoke at length but said little, going on for a half hour, almost succeeding with the afternoon heat in killing those who a half-century before had survived mini balls and cannon fire and bayonets. The men he praised were mostly deaf and, at their distance from the platform, couldn't hear much anyway. Many of them lost interest when they realized they didn't know what he was saying. Others stopped trying to listen when they realized that he didn't know what he was talking about. The former enemies did continue to talk.

"You didn't lose nothin', Yank," the gray barked. "Nothin.'" A bitter glaze had come over the old rebel's eyes. "A few Pennsylvania volunteers who turned and ran, that's all you lost. We lost over five thousand men. We lost ever'thing. We lost the Grand Cause!"

"You lost traitors. Not men." The blue had had enough of shaking hands and smiling for cameras with the old bastard and wished he hadn't helped him climb over the rock wall.

"Traitors?" the old rebel yelled. "You talkin' about your volunteers who hightailed it? They were the traitors. If Armistead would've had another fifty men we'd of crashed Meade's line. Meade would of been handin' his sword to The General. Don't tell me about traitors, you god – damned carpetbagger."

"I ain't no carpetbagger," the blue shouted back. "Only time I was down south was to march through Virginia to Appomattox. Lucky we didn't shoot all you sorry slavers on the spot! How many slaves did you have anyway, Reb?"

"How many niggers fucked your sister, Yank?"

They lunged at each other as best they could—arthritic fingers at each others' throats, dim eyes flashing, unsynchronized shouts of northern aggression and southern treason and faint references to biblical enslavements and the sacred union coughing up through the ball of dust that surrounded the two old men as they wrestled each other to the ground and tried to choke each other with their bony hands.

Up on Cemetery Ridge, at the field hospital, the lieutenant peered through the field glasses toward the crowd down on Hancock Avenue.

"Uh, oh," he called back toward the tent. "I see them loading up an ambulance. Get ready." He could hear the men inside the tent, the privates who had been made nurses and the doctors who had been made surgeon-captains; they were collectively grumbling about the heat and taking up their positions around the dressings cabinets and the triage tables.

The field ambulance made its way up Cemetery Ridge and groaned to a halt in front of the tent. Two medics jumped clear and lifted a blue casualty onto a litter, then carried him inside where they laid him out on the first table. He was at least eighty years old. Captain Benton began to triage the old man.

"Panting," Benton reported as he began see just how bad off he was. "Skin's hot as a skillet. Not sweating. Hey, sir. Sir? Sir? Can you hear me?" he said down to the old man's face. The man just lay there, his skin boiling.

Benton snapped at one of the nurses, a private, to get a thermometer. He peeled back the man's worn out blue uniform and felt around for some bare skin, then stuck a thermometer between his gums. "Sir? What's your name? How do you feel?" Benton looked at his colleague, Captain Trimble, who stood by ready to help. "Sir? What happened?"

The old man spat the thermometer out and wheezed up from the table.

"God Damned bastard! I should have killed him!" the old man sputtered. "Where is he? I'll tear his head off, sonofabitch reb." He more or less waived his bony arm around and exhibited the worn claw with which he would have done the head-tearing if only the reb had been decent enough to hold still. His fusty beard and strands of gray hair poked out of a nearly bald head. His ancient uniform was so tight that Benton had trouble opening the buttons on his collar and front to cool him down. "Jumped me, the bastard!" He waved the claw around a bit more, hoping his nemesis would come within range.

"He's got heat stroke." Benton barked out to the nurses to get all his clothes off and sponge him down with cold water. "If we don't cool him down and hydrate him we could lose him. What happened?" he asked the ambulance driver.

"We was over by that tree close to the rock wall," the driver answered. "A whole bunch of them was standing around after the speeches, shaking hands and posing, and then someone yelled 'MEDIC' and we found them laid out there on the ground. I thought they was dead. The other fellow looked just as bad."

"What other fellow?"

"The other patient." He pointed back toward the field ambulance where the crew was unloading a second old man, a gray, onto a litter. "Him. That wiry old coot was crawling on top of him. Then he just flopped over, right on the spot. It was like they had like a death grip on each other. Had to pry 'em apart."

They laid the gray out on a different table and moved it as far away from the blue as they could. Captain Trimble yelled that this one, too, had intense heat stroke, and ordered his nurse to get his uniform off.

The lieutenant rifled through the patients' belongings and found their reunion identity cards. He wondered if he should send someone off to look for the old mens' personal effects. Blue had been in the Philadelphia Brigade of the 12th Pennsylvania; he was assigned to one of the northern veterans' tents that the quartermaster corps had put up on Cemetery Ridge. Gray was from the 53d Virginia; his tent was further south, nearer the Wheat Field.

"Got to cool this one down," Trimble called out. "One oh three. Badly dehydrated."

"Ice," Benton yelled. "Need some ice. He's fading." He listened for a heartbeat and felt for a pulse.

The nurse cut the buttons off gray's uniform jacket and rubbed cool, wet cloths on his throat and chest. Grey's eyes flickered, unseeing.

"Who in their right minds decided to let them wear their old uniforms at the reunion?" the lieutenant asked.

"The governor," someone answered. "Well, the reunion planning commission decided, but it just did whatever the governor said."

"Ice. Now!" Benton yelled again. "I'm losing him."

"Good," a voice croaked. It was the gray. Someone noticed that he was muttering while the nurses swabbed his face with cold water. "Die, scalawag!"

"You attacked me, you god-damned reb!" groaned the blue from his table. "Coward!" His eyes began to turn milky. Then he gasped. "Unnhhh…"

Benton tried to hold his head up to get some water down his mouth but all he felt was the life draining out of the old blue soldier.

"You damned yank… Unnhhh," Gray moaned out one last excited utterance. Then he, too slipped away.

Both old soldiers died in the hospital tent, each with a look of grim righteousness chiseled into a wrinkled dead face.

Benton closed blue's eyes; Trimble closed gray's. The nurses draped sheets over them. The ambulance attendants went to the two tables and lifted the old enemies onto stretchers to carry them back to the field ambulance, which now had become a hearse. The two carrying gray's body stumbled and knocked his stretcher into the two men carrying blue out of the tent. Blue's body tumbled onto the dirt.

"Watch what you're doing, you stupid cracker!" The men who were picking blue off the ground were from New Jersey and Pennsylvania.

"Cracker my butt, Yank!" yelled one of the men carrying gray. "Let this old gentleman have some dignity. Get out of the way."

The Yanks, instead of picking blue's body off the ground, shoved their stretcher into the crackers who were trying to walk around them. Gray's body fell to the ground as well. The four ambulance attendants squared off at each other. Fists were swung, blows landed. The lieutenant, who was from Oregon, intervened.

"Stop that fighting right now. You four – stand to attention. I'm putting you under arrest! Pick those two men up and put them back on those stretchers! That's an order – what's this?" The lieutenant had bent over the two dead old combatants. "Doctors – come look at this!" He ordered the ambulance attendants to carry the bodies back into the tent, then lifted the sheets to expose their bare necks.

"There's hardly a mark on either one of them." the lieutenant asked. Their skin was already cold to the touch. Their faces showed no trace of heat exhaustion. "The only marks on their bodies are from you four dropping them on the ground. It'll seem fishy to report that two old men who could barely lift their hands could strangle one another to death and."

"They started it," the ambulance men from the north snapped.

"Bull," yelled back the two from the south. "You've been pickin' a fight with us ever since we got to Gettysburg."

"You want a fight?" the two northern men shouted back.

"Shut up, you four! That's an order."

"It was an assault," Benton announced to the lieutenant and anyone else who would listen. "Pure and simple. Trimble's reb strangled my patient." Benton turned to look at Trimble with an air of forensic satisfaction.

"Strangled your patient?" Trimble drawled. "That poor old southern gentleman couldn't strangle a possum. Look at his fingers! Stiff as sticks." Trimble wasn't willing to let anyone, even Benson, defame a poor old Virginia farmer.

Benton arched his back and glared at Trimble.

"You're damned right, strangled. Did you see my poor old soldier's throat when they brought him in?" Benton snapped back in a harsh New England twang. "Your tobacco spit sharecropper had his stiff fingers right around poor old Billy's neck!"

"Poor Billy my ass," Trimble shouted back. "You Yanks push people around like you own the place! If old Johnny there did anything…"

"WE DO OWN THE PLACE!" Benton yelled back. "WE WON THE WAR! Did you forget that, Cornpone?" Benton put his hand on Trimble's chest and shoved.

"WE'LL SEE WHO OWNS WHAT, YOU GOD-DAMNED CARPETBAGGER," Trimble shoved back, and took a swing.

Benton swung back at Trimble. Fists landed. Jaws snapped. Instruments, tables, and cabinets were knocked to the ground.

An adoring nurse who had spent most of 1913 cleaning up after Captain Benton picked up a splint and tried to hit Captain Trimble, calling him the son of a hot-tempered slave-trader. Her blow was blocked by Captain Trimble's own nurse, who called her a 'nigger-lover' and tried to strangle her with a tourniquet. The ambulance attendants shoved them all out of the way and began the fight in earnest.

The bodies of the blue and the gray lay together in a heap, forgotten in the skirmish.

The battle at Gettysburg resumed.

Jack Woodville London

Jack Woodville London was the first Author of the Year in the history of the Military Writers Society of America, and represented MWSA in France, Italy, and Spain in the 2012 Writers on Deck Authors Tour. He is the Director of Education for MWSA and is a member of the Planning Committee.

He has taught at MWSA courses, including courses on Dialogue, Planning the Novel, Research for Fiction, Writing Sounds and Images, Characters, and Story Arc. He also has been a part of multiple panels, including Editing and Acction- versus Character-driven Books. He also teaches one day courses to veterans and writing groups.

His published novels include *French Letters*, *Virginia's War and French Letters*, *Engaged in War*. His third novel in that group has been completed and is at present being managed by his literary agent.

He wrote a non-fiction book, *A Novel Approach*, on the craft of writing. It won the 2014-2015 E-Lit Gold Prize for books on the craft of writing and was featured by Kirkus Reviews.

He has written nine published articles on the craft of writing, dozens of articles on literature and history, and eighty-six book reviews, including many reviews of MWSA member books. He writes a monthly newsletter, First Draft, that includes each month a chapter from his serialized novel, The (very brief) Wartime Diary of Bart Sullivan, Seaman Second Class.

Jack has undergraduate degrees in history from West Texas A&M and law from the University of Texas. He is a diplomate in fiction from the Academy of Fiction, St. Céré, France, and is a graduate student in creative writing at Oxford University.

Photo by Joyce Faulkner

Photo by Pat McGrath Avery

www.ingramcontent.com/pod-product-compliance
Lightning Source LLC
Chambersburg PA
CBHW050815090426
42736CB00021B/3460